The

WILD GAME
COOKBOOK

The
WILD GAME
COOKBOOK

Recipes from North America's

Top Hunting Lodges

Anna and David Kasabian

With Sharon Tully

Food Photography by Glenn Scott

Food Styling by Catrine Kelty

Creative Publishing
international

www.creativepub.com

Creative Publishing
international

Copyright © 2008
Creative Publishing international, Inc.
18705 Lake Drive East
Chanhassen, Minnesota 55317
1-800-328-3895
www.creativepub.com
All rights reserved

President/CEO: Ken Fund
Vice President Sales/Marketing: Peter Ackroyd
Publisher: Bryan Trandem
Executive Managing Editor: Barbara Harold
Production Managers: Laura Hokkanen, Linda Halls
Creative Director: Michele Lanci-Altomare
Senior Design Manager: Brad Springer
Design Managers: Jon Simpson, Mary Rohl
Additional Text: Sharon Tully
Food Photography: Glenn Scott
Food Styling: Catrine Kelty
Book Design: Peter M. Blaiwas, Vern Associates, Inc.
Cover Design: Peter M. Blaiwas, Vern Associates, Inc.

Printed in China
10 9 8 7 6 5 4 3 2 1

Library of Congress Cataloging-in-Publication Data
Kasabian, Anna.
   The Wild Game Cookbook : recipes from North America's top
hunting resorts and lodges / Anna Kasabian, David Kasabian.
      p. cm.
Includes index.
   ISBN-13: 978-1-58923-318-8 (hard cover)
   ISBN-10: 1-58923-318-2 (hard cover)
   1. Cookery (Game) I. Kasabian, David. II. Title.
   TX751.K37 2008
   641.6'91--dc22   2007007257

Acknowledgments

Thanks to all the owners, managers, chefs, and staff members of the wonderful and unique establishments who have contributed to the cookbook.

Many, many thanks to Sharon Tully, who worked so hard to help us make this book happen—and, as usual, did a fantastic job.

Thank you to art director Peter Blaiwas of Vern Associates, Inc. Your great taste, imagination, and diligence packaged the words with the art perfectly.

Special thanks to our photographer, Glenn Scott, and our food stylist, Catrine Kelty, for their inspired work and wonderful energy.

Thank you to our copyeditors, Julia Maranan, and Sandra Smith for all of their help!

Thank you to Livia Cowan, founder and president of Mariposa (www.mariposa-gift.com), for lending us product for our photo shoots.

And finally, thanks to our golden retriever, Amos, who sat quietly by our side while we worked.

Dedication

For brother Bob, and all those cold, early mornings in the duck blind. (DK)

For cousin Phil Tatoian who loves cooking probably as much as hunting. (AK)

DUCK HUNTING IN THE PYMATUNING REGION

Courtesy of Pennsylvania Game Commission

Contents

B & A Series.
On The Moose River

YOU
SON
OF A
GUN

INTRODUCTION

We spent a great deal of time searching for inns, camps, resorts, and ranches that are totally devoted to the sportsman, great food and hospitality.

One by one, as we discovered them, we invited each to contribute to this book by sharing some of their favorite recipes. The response from cooks, chefs, and owners was fabulous, and as you will soon find, so are their recipes.

We want you to use this for the recipes and cooking tips, but we hope too that we have introduced you to some new places to visit with your families, hunting buddies, or colleagues. In the back of the book you will notice a directory of all the contributors, many of which are also Orvis endorsed. Take a look, visit their Web sites, and perhaps you will be inspired as you plan your next hunting trip.

And when you return home, don't forget to pull this off the bookshelf! You will find a full range of recipes here, from simple to complex, from chefs and cooks all over North America—from Georgia to Alaska to British Columbia—all meant to bring you enjoyable feasts with family and friends.

—Anna and David Kasabian

Fillet of Buffalo with Applewood Bacon, Herb-Roasted Fingerling Potatoes, Caramelized Pearl Onions, and Gorgonzola-Sage Cream

serves six

(6- to 8-ounce/170 to 225 g) buffalo fillets

Salt and pepper

4 slices applewood-smoked bacon

½ pound (225 g) pearl onions, peeled

2 tablespoons (28 g) butter

1 teaspoon (4 g) sugar

Herb-Roasted Fingerling Potatoes

2 pounds (900 g) fingerling potatoes

2 tablespoons (30 ml) canola oil

2 tablespoons (5 g) chopped assorted
   fresh herbs

Salt and pepper

Gorgonzola-Sage Cream

2 shallots, minced

1 teaspoon (5 g) butter

2 tablespoons (5 g) chopped fresh sage

½ cup (120 ml) white wine

2 cups (470 ml) heavy cream

2 ounces (57 g) gorgonzola cheese,
   crumbled

Juice of ½ lemon

Salt and pepper

Heat a large (12-inch/30 cm) frying pan over high heat. Season the buffalo fillets with salt and pepper. Add the buffalo fillets to the hot pan and sear all sides until well browned. Wrap bacon around buffalo fillets and return to hot pan. Sear bacon on all sides until bacon is cooked and crisp and the buffalo is cooked to desired doneness. Cover loosely with foil and keep warm until ready to serve. In a frying pan, sauté onions in butter and sugar until golden brown.

Preheat oven to 350°F (180°C). Toss potatoes with oil and herbs. Season with salt and pepper. Roast on baking sheet for 20 to 30 minutes or until brown. Keep warm until ready to serve.

In a covered pan set over low heat, cook shallots in butter until softened but not browned. Add sage and wine. Bring to a boil and reduce by three-fourths. Add cream and reduce by half. Strain through a wire mesh strainer and discard solids. Add gorgonzola and lemon juice and whisk vigorously until smooth, or use an electric blender. Season with salt and pepper.

To serve, place beef, onions, and potatoes on a large platter or individual plates. Spoon the gorgonzola-sage sauce around beef.

Executive Chef Joseph A. Santangini, Amangani Resort, Jackson, Wyoming

Amangani Resort, Jackson, Wyoming

Duck Prosciutto with Caramelized Pears

serves six to eight as an appetizer

Duck prosciutto

2 tablespoons (12 g) whole allspice

1 tablespoon (6.6 g) dill seed

2 tablespoons (12 g) black peppercorns

1 stick cinnamon

1 tablespoon (5 g) whole coriander seeds

½ cup (73 g) brown sugar

½ cup (146 g) kosher salt

2 whole duck breasts, cut in half

Balsamic Glaze

1 cup (235 ml) balsamic vinegar

Caramelized Pears

*2 large ripe pears (Bartlett or Bosc pears
    from Washington State are excellent)*

½ lemon

3 tablespoons (42 g) unsalted butter

½ teaspoon (2 g) sugar

Pinch of ground black pepper

Bring 4 cups (1 liter) of water to a boil. Add all ingredients to water except duck. Turn off heat and allow mixture to cool completely. Submerge duck in water/spice mixture and refrigerate 6 to 8 hours. Remove duck breasts from mixture and pat dry.

Light smoker with cedar chips and bring to 110°F (43°C). Smoke duck breast for 30 minutes. Remove from smoker and cool.

In a small saucepan set over medium-high heat, boil balsamic vinegar until reduced by one-half or until syrupy. Cool and refrigerate until ready to serve.

Peel and core the pears, then cut each one into four wedges. Rub them with lemon juice to keep them from discoloring. Melt butter in a medium (10-inch/25 cm) frying pan set over medium-high heat. Arrange the pears in the pan in a single layer and sprinkle with sugar. Cook 1½ minutes per side. Transfer to plate to cool.

To serve, fan the pears out on a warmed plate. Sprinkle lightly with ground black pepper. Cut very thin slices of Duck Prosciutto and place on plate alongside pear wedges. Drizzle with Balsamic Glaze and serve.

Executive Chef Joseph A. Santangini, Amangani Resort, Jackson, Wyoming

Grilled Venison Chop and Rabbit Sausage with Red Cabbage, Balsamic Vinegar, and Apples

serves two

Red Cabbage, Balsamic Vinegar, and Apples

1 tablespoon (15 ml) olive oil

1 onion, peeled and finely chopped

6 cups (420 g) thinly sliced red cabbage

2 apples, unpeeled, cored and diced into bite-sized pieces

½ cup (120 ml) water

2 tablespoons (30 ml) balsamic vinegar

2 tablespoons (30 ml) red wine vinegar

1 teaspoon (6 g) coarse salt

Venison Chop and Rabbit Sausage

¼ cup (60 ml) extra-virgin olive oil

2 garlic cloves, minced

1 heaping teaspoon (1 g) chopped fresh rosemary

1 (8-ounce/225 g) venison chop

1 tablespoon (5 g) dried green peppercorns

6 ounces (170 g) rabbit sausage

Heat oil in large skillet over medium heat and add onion and cabbage. Sauté until onion is soft, about 5 minutes. Add apples, water, vinegars, and salt. Cook for an additional 20 minutes, or until cabbage is just barely tender. Cover and keep hot until ready to serve.

Place olive oil, garlic, and rosemary in a bowl. Add venison chop and marinate for 30 minutes. Heat grill to high. Remove venison chop from marinade and coat with peppercorns. Grill venison chop for 8 to 10 minutes or until chop is browned on the outside and juicy pink on the inside. Cook sausage until the outside is brown and the juices run clear.

To serve, place some red cabbage mixture on each plate. Cut the grilled venison chop meat away from the bone. Carve meat on the bias into thin slices. Slice rabbit sausage into bite-size pieces. Top each plate with half the grilled venison chop slices and half the rabbit sausage pieces.

Executive Chef Joseph A. Santangini, Amangani Resort, Jackson, Wyoming

Pan-Seared Hudson Valley Foie Gras, Toasted Brioche, Pear-Shallot Compote, and Port Wine–Fig Syrup

serves two

Pear-Shallot Compote
1 tablespoon (14 g) butter
2 ripe pears, peeled, cored and diced
1 shallot, peeled and minced
1 teaspoon (2 g) minced fresh ginger
2 ounces (60 ml) white wine
2 ounces (60 ml) champagne vinegar
2 ounces (60 ml) honey
Salt and pepper

Port Wine–Fig syrup
1 cup (235 ml) port wine
2 dried black figs, minced

Foie Gras
1 teaspoon (5 g) butter
2 (2-ounce/55 g) portions Hudson Valley foie gras (duck liver)
2 (3-inch/7.5 cm) triangles brioche or light yeast bread, crust removed, toasted

Heat a medium (10-inch/25 cm) frying pan set over medium heat. Melt butter and sauté pears, shallot, and ginger until pears are very soft. Add wine, vinegar, and honey. Simmer gently for 10 minutes on medium heat. Season with salt and pepper.

Combine port wine and figs in a small saucepan and simmer until syrupy. Strain through a fine mesh strainer, discarding the solids.

Heat a small (6-inch/15 cm) frying pan set over medium-high heat. Melt butter in the hot pan. While butter is still sizzling, add the foie gras and sear on both sides until light golden brown. The foie gras should be rare.

To serve, spoon some pear-shallot compote in center of each plate. Place brioche on top of compote. Place foie gras on top of brioche. Drizzle port wine–fig syrup around the foie gras.

Executive Chef Joseph A. Santangini, Amangani Resort, Jackson, Wyoming

Five-Spice Peking Duck Breast with Nori with Sticky Rice, and Cilantro Ponzu Sauce

serves two

Peking Duck

2 duck breasts, skin on

Cinnamon, to season

Clove, to season

Fennel seed, to season

Star anise, to season

Black pepper, to season

Nori with Sticky Rice

2 sheets seaweed wrapper (nori)

Sushi rice, seasoned and prepared
*   according to package instructions*

1 small cucumber, peeled, seeded, and
*   sliced into matchsticks*

1 small red bell pepper, cored and sliced
*   into matchsticks*

1 small yellow bell pepper, cored and sliced
*   into matchsticks*

Cilantro Ponzu Sauce

¼ cup (60 ml) soy sauce

2 tablespoons (30 ml) water

1 tablespoon (15 ml) rice wine vinegar

1 ounce (28 ml) fresh orange juice

2 teaspoons (4 g) freshly grated ginger

½ jalapeño, stem and ribs removed,
*   minced*

1 tablespoon (1 g) minced fresh cilantro

Score the skin side of duck breast with a very sharp knife so it will render some fat and the skin will get crispy. Season both sides of duck with five spices.

Heat a cast-iron or other heavy frying pan over medium-high heat. Place the duck breasts into the hot pan skin-side down and cook until skin turns very deep golden brown and some fat has accumulated in the pan. Flip the duck breast over in the pan and cook until medium-rare (the meat is not yet firm but springs back quickly when pressed with a finger) or medium (the meat is somewhat firm to the touch). Keep warm until ready to serve.

Toast and soften the nori sheets by holding briefly over a lit burner on stovetop. Spread sushi rice over the width and one half the length of each nori sheet. Place some cucumber, red bell pepper, and yellow bell pepper slices across the width of the rice. Roll the nori up and over the rice and vegetables, tucking the ends in, to make a tight cylinder. Slice nori rolls on an angle before serving.

In small bowl, combine all sauce ingredients and mix well.

To serve, carve the duck breast into ¼-inch (1 cm) slices, fan them across a platter or serving plates, add the sliced nori rolls, and drizzle the ponzu sauce over the duck and nori rolls and around the plate.

Executive Chef Joseph A. Santangini, Amangani Resort, Jackson, Wyoming

Porcini-Crusted Venison, Yukon Gold Potato and Celery Root Gratin, Wild Mushroom Ragout, and Sauce Perigueux

serves two

Porcini-crusted venison
¼ cup (56 g) porcini mushroom powder
(6- to 8-ounce/170 to 225 g) venison
    sirloin steaks
Salt and pepper

Yukon Gold Potato and
    Celery Root Gratin
1 pound (450 g) Yukon gold potatoes,
    sliced thin
1 pound (450 g) celery root, sliced thin
1 teaspoon (3 g) minced garlic
1 cup (235 ml) heavy cream
¼ cup (20 g) grated asiago cheese
Salt and pepper to taste

Wild Mushroom Ragout
2 tablespoons (30 ml) olive oil
3 tablespoons (30 g) minced shallots
1 pound (450 g) portobello mushrooms, sliced
¼ cup (45 g) finely diced tomatoes
¼ cup (60 ml) vegetable or chicken broth
¼ cup (60 ml) heavy cream
2 tablespoons (5 g) chopped fresh herbs

Sauce Perigueux
1 shallot, chopped
1 sprig thyme
1 tablespoon (14 g) butter
½ cup (120 ml) red wine
3 cups (700 ml) veal or beef stock, reduced
    to ½ cup (120 ml)
Truffle slices (omit if not available)

Preheat grill to high. Sprinkle porcini mushroom powder on venison, season with salt and pepper, and grill to desired doneness. Cover loosely with foil and keep warm until ready to serve.

Preheat oven to 350°F (180°C). Layer sliced potatoes and celery root in a 9 x 13-inch (23 x 33 cm) baking dish. Add garlic and cream, sprinkle with Asiago cheese, and season with salt and pepper. Bake for 45 minutes or until bubbling and potatoes and celery root are tender when pierced with a knife. Cover with parchment paper. Place another pan of approximately the same size over the top and weigh it down with a couple of cans from the pantry. Allow to cool. Cut into square or triangular shapes when ready to serve.

Heat olive oil and shallots in a frying pan set on medium-high heat. Add sliced mushrooms and toss in the pan. Cook mushrooms until soft and fragrant, about 4 minutes. Add tomatoes, broth, heavy cream, and chopped herbs. Cook on medium-high until reduced enough that the sauce coats the back of a spoon. Keep warm.

In a covered sauté pan over low heat, cook shallot and thyme in butter until softened but not browned. Add red wine and reduce by three-fourths. Add stock and reduce. Add sliced black truffles.

To serve, put a slice of potato gratin in the center of each plate and spoon some mushroom ragout on top of gratin. Place steak next to potato gratin on each plate and spoon sauce around the steak.

Executive Chef Joseph A. Santangini, Amangani Resort, Jackson, Wyoming

Prosciutto-Wrapped Pheasant Breast with Root Vegetable Hash, Frisée, and Granny Smith Apple Gastrique

serves four

Prosciutto-Wrapped Pheasant Breasts

4 whole skinless, boneless pheasant breasts

Salt and pepper

4 thin slices prosciutto

Root Vegetable Hash

1 tablespoon (14 g) butter

2 medium sweet potatoes, peeled and diced

2 medium Yukon gold potatoes, peeled and diced

4 medium carrots, peeled and diced

2 medium turnips or rutabagas, peeled and diced

1 shallot, peeled and minced

1 clove garlic, peeled and minced

1 tablespoon (2.5 g) chopped fresh herbs

Granny Smith Apple Gastrique

1 cup (226 g) sugar

⅔ cup (160 ml) cider vinegar

1 cup (235 ml) fresh green apple juice

3 sprigs fresh thyme

4 cups (1 liter) chicken stock

Frisée

¼ pound (115 g) frisée greens, washed and dried

Champagne vinegar, to taste

Salt and pepper

Heat grill to medium. Season pheasant breasts with small amount of salt and pepper. Wrap breasts in prosciutto. Grill on both sides until prosciutto is well-seared and the pheasant is cooked medium-rare (the breast meat will spring back quickly when pressed with a finger). Cover loosely with aluminum foil and keep warm until ready to serve.

Heat butter in a large (12-inch/30 cm) frying pan set over medium heat. Sauté vegetables until soft but not mushy. Add shallot, garlic, and herbs, sauté for 3 minutes longer, stirring gently, and cool.

Melt sugar in a heavy-bottomed pan until it turns golden brown. Add vinegar, apple juice, thyme, and stock. Simmer until mixture thickens slightly.

Season the frisée with a small amount of champagne vinegar, season lightly with salt and pepper.

To serve, divide the root vegetable hash among four plates. Place some dressed frisée on top of hash. Place pheasant breast on each plate and drizzle with gastrique.

Executive Chef Joseph A. Santangini, Amangani Resort, Jackson, Wyoming

Grilled Elk Chop, Roasted Garlic Custard, Oregon Hazelnuts, Winter Squash Ratatouille, and Pan Sauce

serves two

Elk Chops

1 tablespoon (4.3 g) dried juniper berries
1 tablespoon (1.3 g) mixed dried herbs
(like herbs de Provence or fines herbs)
¼ cup (60 ml) olive oil
2 large elk chops
3 cups (705 ml) lamb or beef stock
½ sprig fresh rosemary

Roasted Garlic Custard

2 to 3 cloves garlic
Butter to grease ramekins
1 cup (235 ml) heavy cream
1 egg
1 egg yolk
Salt and pepper

Winter Squash Ratatouille

1 tablespoon (15 ml) olive oil
¼ cup (35 g) finely diced acorn squash
¼ cup (35 g) finely diced butternut squash
¼ cup (20.5 g) finely diced eggplant,
peeled
¼ cup (37 g) finely diced red bell pepper
1 clove garlic, minced
1 shallot, minced
½ cup (90 g) seeded and finely chopped
plum tomato
Mixed herbs of your choice
Salt and pepper
Hazelnuts, chopped and toasted

In a bowl or deep-sided pan combine juniper berries, mixed herbs, and olive oil. Combine well. Add elk chops to the pan and turn to coat completely. Refrigerate, covered, for several hours or overnight. Turn the chops over in the herbed oil every few hours.

Meanwhile, in a small saucepan set on medium, slowly reduce the stock to about ¼ cup (60 ml) or until slightly syrupy. Add the rosemary about 30 minutes before the reduction is done. Keep covered and warm.

Remove elk chops from refrigerator 1 hour before cooking so they warm up to room temperature. Preheat grill to medium-high. Scrape excess oil from elk chops and grill to desired doneness (medium-rare recommended). Keep warm until ready to serve.

Preheat oven to 300°F (150°C). Wrap garlic loosely in a small foil pouch and bake for 40 to 50 minutes, or until garlic is soft. Remove skin and mash with a fork.

Coat two 6-ounce (175 ml) ramekins with butter. Combine roasted garlic purée and remaining ingredients. Pour into buttered ramekins. (There will be a little mixture left over.) Cook in a water bath in oven. Check after 30 minutes. Remove from oven when the centers of the mixture wiggle only slightly when you shake the pan.

Heat oil in a large frying pan over medium-high heat. Sauté the squash, eggplant, red bell pepper, garlic, and shallots for 4 to 5 minutes. Add the tomato and herbs and simmer uncovered until the squash is tender. Season with salt and pepper.

To serve, place some ratatouille on each dinner plate. Place elk chop on top. Run a knife around the inside of the ramekins to loosen the custard; invert onto plate. Sprinkle with hazelnuts and drizzle with pan sauce.

Executive Chef Joseph A. Santangini, Amangani Resort, Jackson, Wyoming

Quail with Braised Greens and Lemon-Thyme Vinaigrette

serves four

Quail
4 boneless quail
Salt and pepper
1 tablespoon (15 ml) vegetable oil

Braised Greens
1 tablespoon (15 ml) olive oil
4 cups (268 g) roughly chopped kale,
    red chard, mustard greens, and
    chicory greens
1 tablespoon (10 g) minced shallot
1 teaspoon (3 g) minced garlic
½ cup (120 ml) chicken stock
Salt and pepper
1 tablespoon (14 g) butter

Lemon-Thyme Vinaigrette
2 tablespoons (20 g) minced shallot
1 teaspoon (3 g) minced garlic
2 tablespoons (5 g) chopped fresh thyme
2 ounces (56 ml) fresh lemon juice
1 teaspoon (5 g) Dijon mustard
2 ounces (56 ml) champagne vinegar
6 ounces (168 ml) olive oil
Salt and pepper

Preheat oven to 400°F (200°C). Season quail with salt and pepper. Heat vegetable oil in a large (12-inch/30 cm) frying pan until barely smoking. Add quail to hot oil and sear until skin is crispy. Transfer to baking sheet and roast in oven until cooked through, about 20 to 25 minutes. Cover loosely with foil and keep warm until ready to serve.

Heat olive oil in a large pot. Add greens and sauté until wilted. Add shallots and garlic and cook for another minute while tossing. Add chicken stock and cook until greens are tender, about 20 minutes. Season with salt and pepper. Add butter and toss.

Combine all vinaigrette ingredients except oil, salt, and pepper. Slowly add oil while whisking vigorously. The mixture will thicken as you go along. Season with salt and pepper.

To serve, spoon braised greens onto a platter, slice quail about ½-inch (1.25 cm) thick and place on top, and spoon some vinaigrette over quail. Serve with mixed grain pilaf or couscous.

Executive Chef Joseph A. Santangini, Amangani Resort, Jackson, Wyoming

Mocha Espresso Flan with Caramel Sauce and English Toffee

serves six

Caramel Sauce

3 cups (600 g) granulated sugar
1 cup (235 ml) water
Dash lemon juice
2 cups (470 ml) whipping cream

English Toffee

2 cups (400 g) sugar
½ pound (225 g) butter
¼ cup (60 ml) water
Vanilla to taste

Flan

3½ cups (822 ml) heavy cream
6 ounces (170 g) granulated sugar
4 egg yolks
3 eggs
1 teaspoon (5g) mocha paste*
¼ cup (60 ml) espresso

* Mocha paste can be found in
  professional-baking-supply houses.
  In a pinch, substitute 1 teaspoon
  (3 g) cocoa.

Combine all Caramel Sauce ingredients except cream in a saucepan and bring to a boil. Continue cooking until the temperature registers 320°F (160°C) on a candy thermometer. Slowly whisk in cream and lower heat. Keep warm until ready to serve.

Combine all toffee ingredients in a saucepan and cook until mixture registers 300°F (150°C) on a candy thermometer. Pour onto rimmed metal baking sheet, cool completely, and chop into small pieces to use as garnish.

For flan, preheat oven to 350°F (180°C). Combine cream and sugar in a saucepan and bring to a boil. Remove from heat and gradually add the egg yolks and eggs while whisking constantly. Mix in mocha paste and espresso.

Spoon mixture into ramekins and place in roasting pan large enough to fit all ramekins without touching. Fill pan with hot tap water so that water comes halfway up the sides of ramekins. Bake until custard is set (approximately 25 minutes). Test by inserting a knife into the center of one flan; it should come out just slightly wet. Cool on countertop, then refrigerate at least 3 hours.

To serve, run a small knife around the edge of each flan to loosen from the ramekins. Invert ramekins onto individual dessert plates and slowly lift away to un-mold flans. Pour caramel sauce over flans and sprinkle with crushed English toffee.

Executive Chef Joseph A. Santangini, Amangani Resort, Jackson, Wyoming

Venison Tenderloin with Sherried Mushrooms

serves four to six

Venison

3 tablespoons (45 ml) olive oil

3 tablespoons (45 ml) liquid smoke

1 tablespoon (18 g) kosher salt

1 tablespoon (7 g) freshly ground
*   black pepper*

2 venison tenderloins

Sherried mushrooms

½ pound (225 g) crimini mushrooms,
*   cleaned and sliced*

4 tablespoons (56 g) butter

Seasoning salt (Alpine Touch or Johnny's
*   Seasoning Salt are recommended, or*
*   combine salt, garlic powder, pepper,*
*   and paprika)*

2 tablespoons (30 ml) sherry cooking wine

3 cups (700 ml) heavy cream

1 pound (450 g) uncooked fettuccine,
*   cooked according to package directions*

In a large bowl, combine olive oil, liquid smoke, salt, and pepper. Marinate tenderloins in mixture for approximately 30 minutes.

Preheat grill to high. Wipe excess marinade from the tenderloins and grill until medium-rare to medium.

In a medium frying pan, sauté mushrooms in butter until well-browned but not dry. Add seasoning salt, sherry, and heavy cream. Mix ingredients and reduce until thick enough to coat the back of a spoon.

Slice venison tenderloins about ½-inch (1.25 cm) thick and place on a bed of fettuccine. Spoon the sherried mushrooms and cream sauce over the tenderloins and fettuccini.

Wine pairing: Lindemans Bin 40 Merlot 2004

Chef Trevor Walter, Big Hole C4 Lodge, Twin Bridges,
Montana

BIG HOLE C4 LODGE, Twin Bridges, Montana

Elk Empanada

makes about sixteen two-bite pastries

2 tablespoons (30 ml) vegetable oil

1½ pounds (680 g) ground elk

½ cup (80 g) finely chopped onion

1 tablespoon (8.5 g) minced garlic

1 tablespoon (18 g) salt

½ tablespoon (3.2 g) pepper

½ tablespoon (1 g) sage

2 tablespoons (30 ml) Worcestershire sauce

1 yam, finely chopped (1½ cups/225 g)

1 apple, finely chopped (1½ cups/165 g)

¼ cup (32 g) cornstarch

1 cup (235 ml) apple cider

12 ounces (355 ml) beer

1 package frozen puff pastry dough

1 egg, beaten

Preheat oven to 400°F (200°C). In a large frying pan set over high heat, heat oil and sauté elk, onion, garlic, salt, pepper, sage, and Worcestershire sauce until elk is cooked and onion is tender. Add yam, apple, cornstarch, apple cider, and beer. Simmer approximately 10 minutes, or until yams are tender. Transfer to a bowl and let cool.

Follow manufacturer's instructions for thawing puff pastry. Cut each puff pastry sheet into 8 squares. Brush the outside edges of the puff pastry squares with beaten egg. Place a heaping tablespoon of elk filling in center of each square and fold over diagonally. Crimp edges with fork to seal. Brush remaining egg on top of pastries. Bake 10 minutes, or until pastry is golden brown.

Serve as hors d'oeuvres, or as a light luncheon with a tossed green salad.

Chef Sue Lomperis, The Lodge and Ranch at Chama Land & Cattle Company, Chama, New Mexico

Wild Turkey and Wild Rice Soup

serves six

2 tablespoons (30 ml) vegetable oil

1 cup (100 g) green onion, finely chopped

1½ cups (180 g) celery, diced

½ cup (74.5 g) red bell pepper, diced

¼ cup (27.5 g) grated carrot

1 to 1½ pounds (450 to 680 g) wild
   turkey breast meat, cut into ½-inch
   (1.25 cm) dice

4 cups (1 liter) water

2 tablespoons (30 ml) chicken bouillon

1 8-ounce (225 g) box long grain and
   wild rice mix, with seasoning

1 large firm apple (Granny Smith works
   well), peeled and cut into ½-inch
   (1.25 cm) dice

In a 4-quart or other large saucepan, heat the vegetable oil and sauté green onion, celery, red bell pepper, and carrots until tender, about 3 minutes. Add wild turkey breast, water, and chicken bouillon. Simmer 15 minutes or until turkey is cooked.

Meanwhile, cook 1 box long grain and wild rice with seasoning. Add cooked rice and apple to soup and simmer for just 5 minutes, until apple is warm but still crisp. Serve immediately.

Variation: Substitute apple with 1½ cups (234 g) sautéed mushrooms and 1 cup (235 ml) heavy cream.

Chef Sue Lomperis, The Lodge and Ranch at Chama Land & Cattle Company, Chama, New Mexico

Grilled Mallard with Plum Sauce

serves four

Plum Sauce

1 (8-ounce/225 g) jar plum jelly

2 tablespoons (31 g) yellow mustard

2 tablespoons (30 g) horseradish

Juice of 1 lemon

Grilled Mallard

1½ to 2 pounds (680 to 907 g) mallard
*   duck breast meat, skin removed*

2 tablespoons (17 g) minced garlic

1 tablespoon (18 g) Greek-style seasoning

1 cup (235 ml) Worcestershire sauce

1 (16-ounce/475 ml) bottle Italian salad
*   dressing*

½ bottle sweet and sour hot sauce
*   (optional)*

Bacon slices, as needed

Seasoned pepper blend (available in
*   supermarkets)*

1 cup (230 g) hickory wood grilling chips,
*   soaked in water at least 1 hour*

Combine sauce ingredients and stir over medium heat until jelly melts. Reserve until ready to serve. Reheat gently before serving.

Rub duck breasts with minced garlic, then sprinkle liberally with Greek seasoning. Combine Worcestershire sauce, Italian dressing, and sweet and sour hot sauce (if using) and pour over duck breasts. Marinate at least 3 hours.

Light charcoal grill with a generous amount of fuel. Wait for the fire to develop an even white ash overall. Just before cooking, tightly wrap 1 slice of bacon around each breast and sprinkle with seasoned pepper. Add a small handful of hickory chips to the fire. Grill with heavy smoke until bacon is golden brown. Breasts are best served medium-rare. Do not overcook. Add more chips if needed. Drizzle plum sauce over grilled breast and serve hot.

Wild rice, asparagus, and spiced apples are recommended side dishes.

Deer Creek Lodge, Sebree, Kentucky

Deer Creek Lodge, Sebree, Kentucky

Grilled Mallard Hors d'oeuvres

Yields about twenty-eight hors d'oeuvres

Plum Sauce

1 (8-ounce/225 g) jar plum jelly

2 tablespoons (31 g) yellow mustard

2 tablespoons (30 g) horseradish

Juice of 1 lemon

Grilled Mallard

*1½ to 2 pounds (680 to 907 g) mallard
    duck breast meat, skin removed*

2 tablespoons (17 g) minced garlic

1 tablespoon (18 g) Greek-style seasoning

1 cup (235 ml) Worcestershire sauce

*1 (16-ounce/475 ml) bottle Italian salad
    dressing*

*½ bottle sweet and sour hot sauce
    (optional)*

Bacon slices, as needed

*Seasoned pepper blend (available in
    supermarkets)*

*1 cup (230 g) hickory wood grilling chips,
    soaked in water at least 1 hour*

Prepare marinade and duck breasts as above, except cut across the grain of the filleted breast to form 1-inch (2.5 cm)-wide strips. Marinate for at least 3 hours, then wrap with slice of bacon and pin with a toothpick. Grill with heavy smoke until bacon turns golden brown. Serve with Plum Sauce to dip in.

*Heavy hickory smoke is imperative when grilling these recipes. The smoke gives the duck a nice flavor, but most important, it adds a golden glaze to the bacon without overcooking it.

Deer Creek Lodge, Sebree, Kentucky

Game Tips

- ■ *The meat of most game birds and animals is significantly lower in saturated fat than that of their domestic counterparts. Quail, pheasant, and guinea hen all have 40 percent fewer calories and 60 percent less fat than chicken.*

- ■ *When you are cooking wild fowl, if the bird isn't young, use a moist-heat method for cooking it. Even if the bird is young, it is a good idea to serve the more-tender breast meat and save the rest for the stock pot to make gravy.*

- ■ *Most people overcook their game because they forget that there is less fat.*

Venison Backstraps with Garlic Sautéed Mushrooms

serves six to ten

Backstraps

Backstraps from 1 deer (1 whole beef
  tenderloin may be substituted)
8 to 10 cloves garlic, peeled and minced
Greek-style seasoning
1 (15-ounce/440 ml) bottle Worcestershire
  sauce
1 cup (235 ml) extra-virgin olive oil
2 (5-ounce/150 ml) bottles hot red pepper
  sauce
1 bottle sweet and sour hot sauce

Garlic Sautéed Mushrooms

2 heaping tablespoons (17 g) minced garlic
½ pound (225 g) butter
½ cup (120 ml) soy sauce
1 pound (450 g) fresh mushrooms, sliced

Thoroughly clean and trim backstraps. Be sure all ligaments and silver skin are removed. Rub liberally with garlic, then sprinkle liberally with Greek-style seasoning and pat into meat. Cut backstraps in half and place in a large container. Sprinkle liberally with Worcestershire sauce, then gently "flood" with olive oil (the olive oil will wash off the Greek seasoning and garlic if you're not careful; you can hold a spoon directly over the meat and flood across the spoon).

Next, pour 2 bottles of hot red pepper sauce and 1 bottle of sweet and sour hot sauce over top of backstraps. Let marinate 1 to 2 hours, then mix meat with marinade to cover thoroughly, and let sit another 30 minutes to 1 hour.

Light charcoal grill with a generous amount of fuel. When the fire is ready, grill the backstraps to your satisfaction (medium-rare to medium recommended).

In a frying pan set over medium heat, combine garlic, butter, and soy sauce. Heat until mixture simmers, then add mushrooms. Sauté to desired texture.

Wild rice, asparagus, and either candied carrots or a pineapple casserole are nice side dishes.

Deer Creek Lodge, Sebree, Kentucky

Goose Pie

serves two to four hungry hunters, or a family of four to six

2 geese, quartered into legs and breasts

½ cup (80 g) chopped onions

4 beef bouillon cubes

1 garlic clove, minced

1 teaspoon (5 ml) Worcestershire sauce

2 tablespoons (3 g) Dymond Lake
    Seasoning (see recipe below)

2 cups (300 g) peeled and diced potatoes

1 cup (128 g) diced carrots

¼ cup (31 g) flour

1 cup (235 ml) cold water

1 (10-inch/26 cm) pie shell, top and
    bottom crusts, uncooked

Dymond Lake Seasoning

1 teaspoon (1.7 g) seasoned pepper
    (available in supermarkets)

1 teaspoon (2 g) celery salt

1 tablespoon (3.8 g) parsley

½ teaspoon (0.9 g) oregano

½ teaspoon (0.7 g) basil

½ teaspoon (0.5 g) thyme

Salt to taste

As testimony to how good this pie is, a hunter named Bernie ate almost two whole goose pies by himself.

Place geese, onions, beef bouillon cubes, garlic, Worcestershire sauce, and Dymond Lake Seasoning in a large Dutch oven and cover with water. Simmer until meat falls off leg bones, about 3 to 4 hours. Let cool, then remove meat from bones. Discard any meat that is still tough. Chop up breasts if they have not already fallen apart. Return meat to broth in Dutch oven and add potatoes and carrots. Cook until vegetables are tender, about 30 minutes.

Preheat oven to 425°F (220°C). Taste to check the seasoning and add a little salt or more Dymond Lake Seasoning if desired. Blend flour into cold water by shaking it in a jar or using a hand blender. Stir into mixture in Dutch oven and simmer while stirring for about 2 minutes. Pour mixture into pie shell. Cover with top crust, cut slits to allow the steam to escape, and bake for 10 minutes. Lower heat to 375°F (190°C) and bake for an additional 40 minutes.

Variation: Add ½ cup (65 g) diced turnips and 1 (10-ounce/ 280 g) can of mushrooms.

Serve with cranberry sauce or a nice chili sauce, tossed salad, and crusty rolls.

This pie freezes very well, baked or unbaked. If unbaked, thaw it before baking and increase the final baking time if necessary—it's best bubbling hot in the middle with a nicely browned crust. If baked before freezing, just heat through until hot and bubbly.

Dymond Lake Lodge, Thompson, Manitoba

Dymond Lake Lodge, Thompson, Manitoba

Spicy Game Chili

serves ten to twelve

---

3 pounds (1.4 kg) game meat
(moose, caribou, venison, elk, or a
combination)

3 tablespoons (45 ml) vegetable oil,
divided

1 cup (235 ml) water

2 medium onions, peeled and sliced thin

2 green peppers, ribs and seeds removed,
cut into strips

2 red bell peppers, ribs and seeds removed,
cut into strips

2 jalapeño chilies, ribs and seeds removed,
finely chopped (optional)

4 garlic cloves, chopped or crushed

2 teaspoons (4.2 g) ground cumin

1 teaspoon (1.8 g) cayenne pepper (or
more to taste)

2 teaspoons (12.6 g) salt

2 cups (475 ml) beef stock

2 (14.5-ounce/410 g) cans crushed or
puréed tomatoes

2 (15-ounce/425 g) cans kidney beans

Cut meat into strips. In a large skillet, heat 2 tablespoons (30 ml) of oil over medium-high heat. Add meat and sauté until strips begin to brown. Add water to pan. Set aside. In a large pot, heat 1 tablespoon (15 ml) of oil. Add onions and cook for 3 minutes. Add peppers, jalapeños, and garlic. Cook another 5 minutes or until softened. Add spices, salt, beef stock, cooked meat, and tomatoes. Bring to a boil. Turn down heat to medium-low and simmer for 1 hour or until meat is tender. Add kidney beans. Simmer for 15 minutes longer.

For thinner chili, add more stock and crushed tomatoes.

Dymond Lake Lodge, Thompson, Manitoba

Handling Your Game

■ *An animal should be eviscerated within an hour of harvest and meat refrigerated within a few hours. Meat will damage or be ruined if it's not dressed, transported, and chilled properly.*

Baked Stuffed Caribou Heart

serves two

1 caribou heart

1 quart (1 liter) cold water

¼ cup (73 g) kosher salt

1 cup (108 g) dry bread crumbs

1 onion, chopped

½ teaspoon (3 g) salt

½ teaspoon (0.75 g) savory or poultry
   seasoning

4 teaspoons (20 ml) melted butter

Salt pork

Wipe heart clean. Combine water and salt in a large pan and soak heart overnight.

Preheat oven to 325°F (170°C). Trim blood vessels and fat from heart. Combine bread crumbs, onion, salt, seasoning, and melted butter to make dressing. Stuff cavity with dressing; skewer or sew up heart. Place in roasting pan and lay strips of salt pork over heart. Add 1 cup (235 ml) water to pan. Cover and bake for 3 hours or until tender.

Flowers River Lodge, Mt. Pearl, Newfoundland

Flowers River Lodge, Mt. Pearl, Newfoundland

BBQ Caribou Ribs

serves four

3 tablespoons (45 ml) cooking oil

4 pounds (1.81 kg) caribou ribs, cut into
  3- or 4-rib pieces

1 cup (235 ml) ketchup

1 cup (235 ml) water

2 tablespoons (30 ml) vinegar

1 tablespoon (15 ml) lemon juice

1 tablespoon (15 ml) Worcestershire sauce

1 tablespoon (15 ml) prepared mustard

3 tablespoons (45 g) brown sugar

1 teaspoon (6 g) salt

¼ teaspoon (0.5 g) pepper

Preheat oven to 350°F (180°C). In a large frying pan, heat oil until barely smoking. Add ribs and sauté until brown. Transfer ribs to a greased baking dish. Add remaining ingredients to pan and bring to boil for 1 minute. Pour mixture over ribs. Cover with foil and bake until tender, about 2 hours.

Flowers River Lodge, Mt. Pearl, Newfoundland

Where's It From and What's It Taste Like?

■ *Caribou (reindeer) live primarily in North America and Siberia. Their meat is sweeter than that of other venison.*

Bourbon Buffalo Pheasant Strips

serves two

½ *yellow onion, diced*

2 *tablespoons (28 g) butter*

¼ *cup (60 ml) bourbon*

⅓ *cup (75 g) brown sugar*

⅔ *cup (160 ml) Frank's Red Hot Sauce or other hot red pepper sauce*

1 *cup (125 g) flour*

1 *tablespoon (18 g) salt*

1 *teaspoon (2 g) black pepper*

4 *to 5 skinless pheasant breasts*

Oil for frying

Ranch or blue cheese dressing for dipping

Place onion and butter in frying pan and cook over medium-high heat until onions become translucent (approximately 3 minutes). Remove pan from heat and add bourbon. Ignite with match or lighter and let flames subside.

Return pan to stove. Stir in brown sugar and cook on low heat until sugar has dissolved. Add hot red pepper sauce and simmer on low heat for a few minutes.

Combine flour, salt, and black pepper in a shallow bowl or pan. Check pheasant breasts for shot. Cut breasts into strips (approximately 5 per breast). Dredge the strips in seasoned flour.

Heat oil 2 inches (5 cm) deep in large heavy-bottomed pan to 360°F (185°C) or until a small piece of bread fries instantly when dropped into the oil. Shake excess flour off pheasant strips and fry in oil until golden brown. Toss strips with bourbon sauce and serve with ranch or blue cheese dressing for dipping.

Chef Matthew Currey, Flying B Ranch, Kamiah, Idaho

FLYING B RANCH, Kamiah, Idaho

Grilled Pheasant Breast over Parmesan Potato Risotto with Spiced Wine Demi-Glace

serves six

Spiced Wine Demi-Glace

½ bottle (375 ml) port wine

½ bottle (375 ml) red wine

2 (14-ounce/395 ml) cans beef broth

2 cinnamon sticks

2 ounces (55 g) orange juice concentrate, thawed

2 packets beef gravy mix

Potato Risotto

6 medium russet potatoes, peeled and diced into very small cubes

Water for boiling, lightly salted

2 tablespoons (28 g) butter

1 pint (475 ml) heavy cream

Salt and pepper

1 cup (80 g) shredded Parmesan cheese

Fresh herbs (optional)

Pheasant Breast

12 boneless, skinless pheasant breasts

2 tablespoons (28 g) butter, softened

Salt and pepper

Bring port wine and red wine to a boil and reduce by three-fourths. Add beef broth, cinnamon sticks, and orange juice. Bring to a boil. Add gravy mix slowly until sauce begins to thicken. (It may not be necessary to use all of mix.) Reduce heat and simmer 15 minutes or to desired thickness. Remove cinnamon sticks and keep sauce covered in a warm place until ready to use.

In a large pot, place potatoes in lightly salted water to cover and bring to a simmer. Cook potatoes until al dente, remove from heat, and drain. Run cold water over the potatoes to stop the cooking. Place butter in a large sauté pan on medium-high heat and add potatoes. Sauté potatoes a few minutes, stirring only once or twice, and then add heavy cream. Add salt and pepper to taste and reduce cream until it begins to thicken. Toss in Parmesan cheese and heat until thickened and well combined. Add fresh herbs like rosemary or thyme if desired. Remove from heat and serve immediately.

Preheat grill to medium. Brush pheasant breast with softened butter and season with salt and pepper. Place on hot grill. (You may sear in frying pan if grill is not available.) Grill pheasant until done, about 3 minutes per side, making sure not to overcook. Serve immediately over potato risotto and drizzle with spiced wine sauce. Serve with vegetable of your choice.

Chef Matthew Currey, Flying B Ranch, Kamiah, Idaho

Maple-Glazed Bacon-Wrapped Chukar

serves six

12 chukar breasts *(pheasant may be*
substituted, but use 6 to 8 breasts)
12 to 14 strips thick-cut smoked bacon
½ cup (120 ml) pure maple syrup

Preheat oven to 400°F (200°C). Cut each chukar in half lengthwise, yielding 24 pieces. Cut the bacon strips in half and wrap each piece of chukar. It may be necessary to fold the chukar in half so that it fits into the bacon when wrapped up. Place wrapped chukar on greased or parchment paper–covered baking sheet. Bake in oven until bacon is nearly done (meat will feel firm but springy when pressed with a finger).

Remove from oven and brush each piece with maple syrup. Place back in oven and bake until finished, about 5 more minutes (remove before syrup begins to burn). Brush once more with syrup and let cool slightly. Serve on platter with frilly toothpicks.

Chef Matthew Currey, Flying B Ranch, Kamiah, Idaho

Spicy Elk and Lentil Stew

serves six

8 slices thick-cut smoked bacon, diced

1 pound (0.5 kg) cubed elk, deer, or
    venison top round

1 medium onion, chopped

2 chipotle peppers in adobo sauce
    (available from gourmet supermarkets)

1 (14½-ounce /410 g) can diced tomatoes

1 celery rib, diced

1 carrot, diced

3 garlic cloves, minced

Salt and pepper to taste

4 tablespoons (60 ml) olive oil

2 packed tablespoons (28 g) light brown
    sugar

2 tablespoons (15 g) chili powder

1 tablespoon (7 g) paprika

2 teaspoons (5 g) ground cumin

½ teaspoon (1 g) cayenne pepper, or to
    taste

2 teaspoons (2 g) dried oregano, crumbled

1 sprig fresh or ½ teaspoon (0.5 g) dried
    thyme

1 (6-ounce/170 g) can tomato paste

1 teaspoon (4 g) dry mustard

2 cups lentils (284 g), rinsed and drained

3 bay leaves

8 cups (2 liters) chicken stock or low-
    sodium chicken broth

Cook bacon in 5- to 6-quart (5- to 6-liter) pot over medium-high heat until fat melts. Add cubed elk and cook for 5 minutes, stirring occasionally. Add onion, chipotle peppers, tomatoes, celery, carrots, garlic, salt, pepper, and oil, stirring occasionally, until vegetables soften (approximately 5 minutes).

Meanwhile, stir together brown sugar, chili powder, paprika, cumin, cayenne pepper, oregano, thyme, tomato paste, and mustard. Add mixture to pot and cook, stirring gently until fragrant (approximately 4 minutes). Add lentils, bay leaves, and stock. Simmer uncovered, stirring occasionally, until lentils are very soft (approximately 50 to 60 minutes). Discard bay leaves before serving.

Chef Matthew Currey, Flying B Ranch, Kamiah, Idaho

Peppered Grilled Elk Medallions with Red Wine Sauce and Lingonberry Compote

serves six

Red Wine Sauce

1 (750 ml) bottle red wine
2 (14-ounce/425 ml) cans beef broth
1 to 2 packets beef gravy mix
1 fresh rosemary sprig

Lingonberry Compote

2 cups (500 g) frozen lingonberries
(lingonberries may be available at
gourmet supermarkets; another berry
may be substituted)
1 (6-ounce/175 ml) can pineapple juice
½ to 1 cup (100 to 200 g) granulated
sugar
3 tablespoons (24 g) cornstarch, mixed
with an equal amount of water (45
ml) to make a paste

Grilled Elk

3 pounds (1.4 kg) elk, deer, or venison top
round, cleaned thoroughly
Salt
Cracked black pepper

Bring red wine to a boil in a 2-quart (1.9 liter) saucepan and reduce by three-fourths. Add beef broth and bring back to a boil. Slowly whisk the gravy mix into the broth until it begins to thicken. (It may not be necessary to use all of the mix.) Reduce heat and simmer 15 to 20 minutes, letting it thicken slowly. Once the mixture reaches the desired consistency, remove from heat. Place rosemary sprig into sauce. Set aside in warm place until needed.

Bring lingonberries and pineapple juice to a boil in a 2-quart (1.9 liter) saucepan. Add ½ cup (100 g) sugar, stir to combine, and reduce heat. Taste to determine if more sugar is necessary. Once compote is to taste, whisk in small amounts of cornstarch mixture until compote thickens a little. (It may not be necessary to use all of the cornstarch mixture.) Simmer gently for 10 minutes to thicken to desired consistency. Remove and cool.

Preheat grill to high. Cut elk into 3- to 4-ounce (85 to 115 g) medallions and sprinkle salt and cracked black pepper on both sides of meat. Grill elk on hot grill to desired doneness. When ready, serve over pool of red wine sauce and top with lingonberry compote. Serve with your favorite vegetable and starch. Scalloped potatoes or roasted red bliss potatoes are a nice accompaniment.

Wine pairing: A full-bodied Cabernet Sauvignon or red Zinfandel is a complementary wine choice.

Chef Matthew Currey, Flying B Ranch, Kamiah, Idaho

Fried Alligator

serves ten

5 pounds (2.5 kg) alligator tail, cut into
   ½-inch (1.25 cm) pieces
8 cups (2 liters) milk
¾ cup (175 ml) bottled Italian dressing
4 tablespoons (60 ml) liquid crab boil
   (available from Cajun grocers)
½ cup (120 ml) hot red pepper sauce
2 teaspoons (10 g) prepared mustard
2 tablespoons (10 g) Creole-style
   seasoning mix
2 teaspoons (6 g) garlic powder
1 cup (235 ml) red wine vinegar
Flour (or fish fry) for dredging
Peanut oil for frying

Mix all ingredients except flour and oil thoroughly in bowl, making certain alligator meat is covered in sauce. Refrigerate at least 24 hours. Drain meat well and roll in flour or fish fry. Heat about 1 tablespoon (15 ml) peanut oil in a frying pan over medium-high heat and fry meat until golden brown and cooked through. Cook in batches, wiping pan out with paper towel between batches.

Golden Ranch Plantation, Gheens, Louisiana

GOLDEN RANCH PLANTATION, *Gheens, Louisiana*

Alligator Sauce Picante

serves four to six

1½ teaspoons (9 g) salt

1 teaspoon (2 g) cayenne pepper

1 teaspoon (2 g) black pepper

⅓ cup (42 g) flour

2 to 3 pounds (1 to 1.5 kg) alligator meat,
    cleaned and cubed

Cooking oil as needed

1 onion, finely chopped

1 (8-ounce/225 g) can diced tomatoes

Water

½ cup (50 g) chopped green onions

½ cup (30 g) chopped parsley

Combine salt, cayenne pepper, black pepper, and flour in a large bowl. Toss alligator meat in flour mixture to coat.

Heat a few tablespoons oil in heavy Dutch oven until smoking and add flour-coated alligator meat. Do not crowd the pan. Cook in batches if needed. The meat will become watery at first; continue cooking over high heat until all water evaporates. Fry until light brown. Transfer meat to another bowl and keep warm until all the alligator meat is cooked.

Add onion to the pan and sauté until translucent. Add tomatoes and cook for 5 minutes. Add water if the mixture becomes too dry. Return the alligator meat to the pan and toss with vegetables. Add green onions and parsley.

Serve over hot cooked rice.

Chef Gayle Fontenot, Grosse Savanne Waterfowl & Wildlife Lodge, Lake Charles, Louisiana

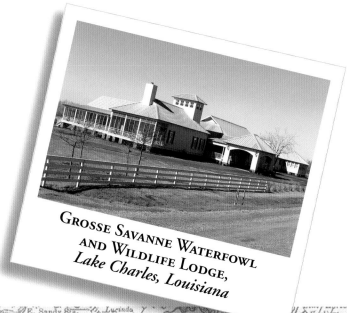

GROSSE SAVANNE WATERFOWL AND WILDLIFE LODGE, Lake Charles, Louisiana

Elk Enchiladas

serves eight to ten

1 pound (450 g) ground elk
1 medium onion, chopped
Salt and pepper
8 to 10 (8-inch/20 cm) flour tortillas
1 (15-ounce/425 g) can chili without
    beans
2 (12 ounce/340 g) cans tomato sauce
3 cups (340 g) shredded four-cheese
    Mexican blend or Colby/Jack cheese

Preheat oven to 350°F (180°C). In a large (12-inch/30 cm) frying pan set over high heat, brown ground elk and onions, season with salt and pepper, drain, and set aside.

Wrap flour tortillas in a dish towel and warm in microwave a few seconds. Mix chili and tomato sauce in large glass or ceramic bowl. Microwave for 1 minute.

Pour some chili mixture in bottom of 9 x 13-inch (23 x 33 cm) baking dish. Fill each tortilla with heaping tablespoon of meat mixture and top with equal amount of cheese. Roll up and place seam-side down in baking dish. Repeat until dish is full. Pour remaining chili mixture over enchiladas and top with remaining cheese. Bake for about 30 minutes or until bubbly.

Chef Kim Souther, Heartland Wildlife Ranches, Ethel, Missouri

HEARTLAND WILDLIFE RANCHES
Ethel, Missouri

Game Meatballs

serves six to eight

Meatballs

3 pounds (1.4 kg) ground game meat (elk,
   buffalo, and/or deer are recommended)

1 (12-ounce/355 ml) can evaporated milk

1 cup (80 g) rolled oats (oatmeal)

1 cup (50 g) cracker crumbs of your choice

2 eggs

½ cup (80 g) chopped onions

½ tablespoon (4 g) garlic powder

2 tablespoons (36 g) salt

½ tablespoon (3 g) ground black pepper

2 tablespoons (15 g) chili powder

Sauce

2 cups (470 ml) ketchup

1 cup (220 g) brown sugar

½ teaspoon (2.5 ml) liquid smoke

½ teaspoon (1.5 g) garlic powder

¼ cup (40 g) chopped onions

Preheat oven to 350°F (180°C). Combine all meatball ingredients. Mix gently to incorporate. Do not overmix. Make into golf ball–sized meatballs. Place in greased baking dish.

Combine sauce ingredients, mix well, and pour over meatballs. Bake in preheated oven for 1 hour.

Chef Kim Souther, Heartland Wildlife Ranches, Ethel, Missouri

Game Marinade

makes enough for 3- to 4-pounds (1.4 to 1.8 kg) meat

½ cup (120 ml) olive oil

½ cup (120 ml) white wine

½ cup (120 ml) soy sauce

4½ (67 ml) tablespoons honey

6 large garlic cloves, minced

3 tablespoons (5 g) chopped fresh rosemary,
   or 1 tablespoon (3 g) dried

1½ tablespoons (10 g) coarsely ground
   black pepper

1½ tablespoons (27 g) sea salt

Combine all ingredients in a large resealable plastic bag and mix well. Add meat to bag. Push out excess air, seal, and refrigerate for several hours or overnight.

This simple marinade can be used with your favorite game, whether you roast, grill, or sauté.

Chef Kim Souther, Heartland Wildlife Ranches, Ethel, Missouri

Native Game in North America

Big Game	Small Game	Game Birds
antelope	alligator	grouse
bear	armadillo	guineafowl
buffalo	beaver	partridge
caribou	muskrat	pheasant
deer	opossum	quail
elk	porcupine	squab (young pigeon)
moose	rabbit	wild ducks
reindeer	raccoon	wild geese
wild boar	squirrel	wild turkey

Smothered Elk Steaks

serves four

4 (8-ounce/227 g) elk strip steaks
Salt and pepper
Flour for dredging
1 tablespoon (15 ml) vegetable oil
12 ounces (336 ml) Chardonnay
2 (10.75-ounce/305 g) cans cream of
   mushroom soup
1 envelope beef-flavored dry onion soup
1 large onion, sliced very thin, rings
   separated
Several fresh mushrooms, sliced

Using a very sharp knife, cut crisscross patterns about ⅛-inch (3 mm) deep on both sides of steaks. Season with salt and pepper. Dredge in flour, being sure to shake off excess flour.

Heat vegetable oil in a nonstick frying pan (an electric skillet can be used) and brown the steaks thoroughly on both sides. After the second side has browned, add half the wine and boil for 3 to 4 minutes. Mix soups together with remaining wine. Add this to top of steaks, cover with onion rings and mushrooms, then cover pan and let simmer for 2 to 3 hours, or until steaks are tender.

Mashed potatoes, seasoned green beans, and warm hot rolls make great accompaniments.

Chef Kim Souther, Heartland Wildlife Ranches
Ethel, Missouri

Where's It From and What's It Taste Like?

■ *Elk are from North America, Europe, and Asia. The meat is mild
and similar to beef but with a bit of a sweet flavor and a faint
taste of deer venison. You can easily substitute elk in recipes that
call for deer venison.*

Grilled Axis Venison with Green Peppercorn Sauce

serves six to eight

3 to 3½ pounds (1.4 to 1.6 kg) venison,
   backstrap, or ham
Salt and pepper
3 to 4 cloves garlic, peeled and minced

Green Peppercorn Sauce
½ cup (112 g) butter
½ cup (80 g) chopped red onion
½ cup (30 g) chopped fresh parsley
2 teaspoons (6 g) minced garlic
2 teaspoons (3 g) green peppercorns
2 tablespoons (13 g) seasoned pepper
   (available in supermarkets)
⅔ cup (157 ml) red wine
1½ cups (350 ml) water
1 cup (235 ml) half-and-half

Cut venison into serving-size pieces, being sure to remove all silver skin. Season with salt and pepper and rub with garlic. Cover and refrigerate for several hours.

Preheat grill to high. Grill venison to medium-rare, about 6 to 15 minutes (depending on thickness). Remove venison from grill and let it sit for 5 minutes before proceeding. Thinly slice meat on the bias, three-fourths of the way through.

Melt butter in large saucepan over medium heat. Add onion and cook until it becomes translucent. Add parsley, garlic, and peppercorns. Add pepper and stir until smooth. Add wine and water and bring to a boil, then add half-and-half. Stir over low heat until smooth and thick. Pour over venison and serve.

Joshua Creek Ranch, Boerne, Texas

JOSHUA CREEK RANCH, Boerne Texas

Pheasant Amaretto

serves two

2 whole boneless pheasant breasts

Flour, seasoned with salt, pepper, and a
  pinch of thyme, for dredging

4 tablespoons (56 g) unsalted butter

1 fluid ounce (29 ml) amaretto

½ cup (120 ml) heavy cream

1 fluid ounce (29 ml) white
  wine (Chardonnay works well)

¼ cup (23 g) sliced almonds, toasted on a
  baking sheet in a 350°F (180°C) oven
  for 10 minutes

Preheat oven to 325°F (165°C). Flatten pheasant breasts slightly and dust with seasoned flour. Heat butter in frying pan until bubbling subsides and brown pheasant breasts on both sides. Transfer pheasant breasts to platter, cover loosely with foil, and put in oven to keep warm while making sauce.

Return pan to medium heat. Gradually whisk amaretto, heavy cream, and wine into the drippings in the pan. Simmer until liquid is thick enough to coat the back of a spoon.

Remove pheasant from oven. Pour sauce over warm pheasant, top with almonds, and serve immediately with wild rice.

Joshua Creek Ranch, Boerne, Texas

Elk Hanger Steak with Charred Eggplant and Goat Cheese Purée and Black Radish Salad

serves four

2 whole elk hanger steaks (approximately
    12 to 16 ounces each)
Marinade (recipe follows)
1 medium black radish (red radish may
    be substituted)
½ lemon
Salt and pepper
1 medium eggplant
4 ounces (113 g) fresh goat cheese
2 tablespoons (6 g) chopped chives

Marinade

¼ cup (60 ml) warm water
1 teaspoon (6 g) fine sea salt
¼ cup (60 ml) tamari sauce
½ teaspoon Espelette or other dried red
    chili pepper
1 teaspoon (5 ml) amber agave syrup
    (available from Mexican grocers, or
    substitute light corn syrup)

Clean steaks of any excess sinew, fiber, or silver skin. Separate the two lobes along center line of sinew, leaving 4 steaks (two will be slightly thicker than the other two). Whisk together the marinade ingredients and pour into large resealable plastic bag. Add steaks to marinade and refrigerate, turning every 30 minutes for 1 to 4 hours before cooking.

Scrub radish under cold running water to remove any dirt or grit. Thinly slice into rounds, then slice rounds lengthwise into matchsticks. Place radish in a bowl and squeeze lemon over it. Season with salt and pepper and toss well. Cover and set aside at room temperature.

Preheat grill to medium. Poke a few holes in the eggplant with a paring knife or toothpick and place on hot grill. Cook on all sides until completely charred and tender. Remove to a bowl and let cool for 10 minutes. Once eggplant is cool enough to handle, peel off the charred skin, using a paring knife when necessary. Purée warm eggplant and goat cheese in food processor until smooth. Season with salt and pepper.

Remove steaks from marinade and pat dry. Season very lightly with salt and place on hot grill. Grill for 5 minutes on each side for rare to medium-rare meat, longer if well done is preferred. Let meat rest on a warm plate for 5 minutes before serving. While meat is resting, heat eggplant purée to a simmer in small pot. Add chives to radish salad and toss well.

To serve, slice steak diagonally across the grain, cutting pieces 1-inch (2.5 cm) thick. Place a large spoonful of purée in center of each plate. Top with several slices of steak, and arrange radish salad on top.

Keyah Grande, Pagosa Springs, Colorado

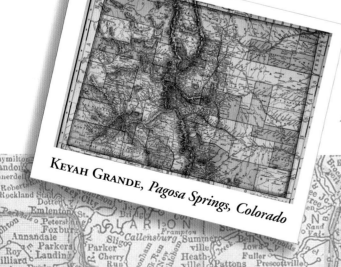

KEYAH GRANDE, *Pagosa Springs, Colorado*

Open Fire–Roasted Corn and Grilled Jicama Salad

serves six

2 ears of corn, husks on

1 cup (120 g) peeled jicama, sliced into
thick rounds

2 tablespoons (30 ml) olive oil, divided

Salt and pepper to taste

1 cup (150 g) chopped red or orange bell
pepper

3 green onions, sliced

⅓ cup (5 g) chopped fresh cilantro

2 tablespoons (30 ml) fresh lime or
lemon juice

¼ to ½ teaspoon (1 to 2.5 ml) hot red
pepper sauce, or to taste

¼ teaspoon (1.5 g) salt

6 large red leaf, romaine, or iceberg lettuce
leaves, or corn tortilla chips

Preheat grill to medium-high. Roast corn in husks over grill, turning frequently, until kernels are tender and fragrant. Let cool and cut the corn kernels from cob. Brush jicama slices with 1 tablespoon (15 ml) oil, sprinkle with salt and pepper, and grill just enough to create grill marks. Dice jicama into kernel-sized pieces. Combine the corn, jicama, bell pepper, onions, and cilantro in a medium bowl. In another bowl, whisk together lime juice, 1 tablespoon (15 ml) oil, hot red pepper sauce, and salt, and pour over corn mixture. Toss well, cover, and chill at least 1 hour to allow flavors to blend. Serve wrapped in lettuce leaves or with corn tortilla chips.

Lajitas, the Ultimate Hideout, Lajitas, Texas

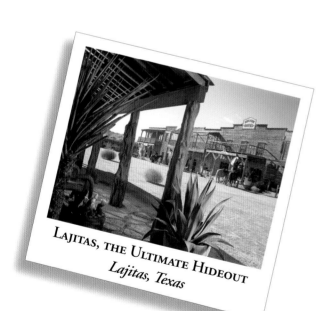

LAJITAS, THE ULTIMATE HIDEOUT
Lajitas, Texas

Palo Amario Potato-Wrapped Breast of Wild Turkey with Roasted Red Pepper Aioli

serves two

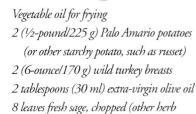

Vegetable oil for frying

2 (½-pound/225 g) Palo Amario potatoes (or other starchy potato, such as russet)

2 (6-ounce/170 g) wild turkey breasts

2 tablespoons (30 ml) extra-virgin olive oil

8 leaves fresh sage, chopped (other herb may be used)

8 leaves fresh Italian parsley, chopped (other herb may be used)

Salt and pepper to taste

¼ cup (60 ml) mayonnaise

Juice of ½ lemon

2 small roasted red bell peppers, skinned and seeded (or small jar of roasted peppers, drained well)

Paprika to taste

Fresh sage leaves and parsley for garnish

Heat vegetable oil to 350°F (180°C) in a large, heavy-bottomed pan, filling no more than one-third the depth of the pan. Peel potatoes, then slice very thin lengthwise (use a mandoline, if you have one). You should get six slices, each about ¼-inch (6 mm) thick. Deep-fry potatoes until barely cooked and pliable. Place on paper towels to drain.

Place turkey breasts in mixing bowl and add olive oil, sage, parsley, salt, and pepper to taste. Marinate for 5 minutes. Heat a large frying pan on high heat. Sear turkey breast on both sides just enough to give them a golden-brown color. Set aside to cool.

Preheat oven to 350°F (180°C). Wrap the turkey breasts with the potato slices, securing with toothpicks if necessary. Place on greased baking sheet and bake in oven for about 12 to 15 minutes or until the potato is golden brown and the turkey breast registers 160°F (71°C) on an instant-read thermometer inserted into the thickest part of the meat. Cover loosely with foil to keep warm until ready to serve.

Place mayonnaise, lemon, and roasted red pepper in a food processor or blender and blend until pepper is fully incorporated into the mayonnaise. Add paprika, salt, and pepper to taste.

To serve, place potato-wrapped turkey on individual dinner plates. Drizzle with Roasted Red Pepper Aioli. Garnish with fresh sage leaves and parsley and serve with vegetables and rice, if desired.

Lajitas, the Ultimate Hideout, Lajitas, Texas

Deer Liver and Onions

serves four

1 deer liver
Milk to cover liver
1 pound (450 g) bacon (more if desired)
2 large onions, chopped
2 cups (470 ml) ketchup
Flour for dredging
2 tablespoons (30 ml) cooking oil

Slice liver, removing any bloodshot parts. Marinate in milk in refrigerator for several hours. When ready to cook, heat a frying pan over medium-high heat. Fry bacon until crisp; add onions and fry until nice and brown. Put onions and bacon in saucepan and add ketchup to make sauce. Keep warm. Place flour in a shallow pan or bowl and dredge liver in flour. Heat oil in bottom of large cast-iron skillet and place liver in skillet to cook quickly. Transfer to serving platter. Cover with sauce and serve.

Libby Camps Sporting Lodges and Outfitter, Ashland, Maine

LIBBY CAMPS, SPORTING LODGES AND OUTFITTER, *Ashland, Maine*

Moose/Deer Mincemeat

yields filling for two 10-inch (25 cm) pies

1 to 1½ pounds (450 to 675 g) deer and/
    or moose meat, cut into large chunks

Water to cover meat (or use broth)

3 heaping cups (350 g) ground apples

½ cup (225 g) beef suet

1½ cups (355 ml) vinegar

1 tablespoon (6 g) allspice

1 tablespoon (7 g) nutmeg

2 tablespoons (14 g) cinnamon

½ teaspoon (1 g) ground cloves

2 cups (300 g) raisins

1 cup (235 ml) molasses

1 teaspoon (6 g) salt, or to taste

2½ cups (500 g) sugar, or to taste

In a small pot, simmer meat in water until cooked through, about 30 minutes. Remove meat from water to cool, and reserve the cooking water, skimming and discarding any fat that may rise to the top. Grind meat in a meat grinder.

Preheat oven to 350°F (180°C). Mix meat, reserved cooking water, and remaining ingredients together. Roast for 1 to 2 hours or until most of the water has cooked off. (To cook on stovetop, omit most of the water and stir frequently.) May be frozen or canned.

Libby Camps Sporting Lodges and Outfitter, Ashland, Maine

What Influences the Quality of the Meat?

■ *Factors that determine quality are age, diet, and the time of the year the animal was harvested. Fall is the best time to hunt because it follows the spring and summer, when food was plentiful.*

Slow-Cooked Goose

serves four to six

½ cup (120 ml) soy sauce

4 teaspoons (20 ml) oil

4 teaspoons (20 ml) lemon juice

2 teaspoons (10 ml) Worcestershire sauce

1 teaspoon (3 g) garlic powder

2 pounds (0.9 kg) goose breast, cubed

¾ cup (94 g) flour

¼ cup (56 g) butter

1 (10.75-ounce/305 g) can cream of
    mushroom soup

1⅓ cup (313 ml) water

1 envelope onion soup mix

In glass bowl or resealable plastic bag, combine soy sauce, oil, lemon juice, Worcestershire sauce, and garlic powder. Add goose and marinate several hours in refrigerator.

Place flour in a shallow pan and coat goose breast on all sides. Heat butter in a frying pan and brown goose on all sides. Transfer goose to a slow cooker. Add cream of mushroom soup, water, and onion soup mix. Cook on high for 4 to 5 hours or until meat is tender. If you don't have a slow cooker, use a heavy (such as cast-iron) covered pot and bake in 200°F (93°C) oven for 3 to 4 hours.

Serve over mashed potatoes, rice, or noodles.

Libby Camps Sporting Lodges and Outfitter, Ashland, Maine

Speaking of Goose…

- *It's got a lot of fat right under the skin, not in the meat, so be prepared to see a lot of fat melt out during roasting.*
- *Consider scalding and drying the goose before you cook it so the skin tightens and squeezes out the fat.*
- *Since there's not much meat on a goose, it is a good idea to stuff it.*
- *It is not as easy to carve as a chicken, so carve it in the kitchen— not at the table.*
- *Goose parts can be substituted in any recipe calling for duck breasts or legs.*

Deer Ham

serves eight to ten with leftovers

1 (5- to 6-pound/2.3 to 2.7 kg) deer ham
1 cup (235 ml) water
1 cup (235 ml) diet cola
1 cup (235 ml) barbeque sauce

Preheat oven to 190°F (88°C). Place deer ham in a large, heavy pot. Add 1 cup (235 ml) water. Cook in oven 12 hours, checking every few hours to make sure there's still a little liquid on the bottom of the pan. If not, add a little bit of water and keep cooking.

Drain juices and remove fat and bones. Add diet cola and barbeque sauce to pot. Cook for 6 more hours.

Lily Pond Creek Hunting Lodge, Jackson, North Carolina

Venison Defined

■ *Venison includes meat from deer, elk, moose, caribou, antelope, and pronghorn. If you choose to purchase it from a store, look for the specific name of the animal on the label.*

Lily Pond Creek Hunting Lodge
Jackson, North Carolina

Pancakes

serves four

2 cups (250 g) flour
1 teaspoon (5 g) baking soda
2 tablespoons (12 g) sugar
1 teaspoon (6 g) salt
2 cups (470 ml) buttermilk
2 tablespoons (30 ml) oil
2 eggs, separated into yolks and whites.
2 teaspoons (2 g) ground cinnamon
2 tablespoons (28 g) butter, or as needed

In a large bowl, combine flour, baking soda, sugar, salt, and buttermilk and mix gently to combine. Add oil and egg yolks and mix gently to combine. In a separate bowl, beat egg whites until frothy, then beat in cinnamon and fold into flour mixture.

Heat a large frying pan or griddle on burner set to medium. Add 1 teaspoon (5 g) of butter and spread it around as it melts to coat pan bottom. Ladle batter into pan, about ¼ cup (60 ml) per pancake, and cook until bubbles form all over the top of the batter. Flip the cakes over in the pan and cook another minute or until golden brown. Remove from pan and keep warm. Repeat until all the batter is used. Serve hot with maple syrup, fruit, or other topping.

Lily Pond Creek Hunting Lodge, Jackson, North Carolina

Grilled Stuffed Quail with Buttered Apples and Wilted Spinach

serves six

6 boned quails

Salt and pepper

1 tablespoon (2 g) chopped fresh thyme

1 cup (195 g) cooked brown rice

½ cup (80 g) chopped apricots

8 slices smoked bacon, chopped and
    cooked (discard fat)

2 tablespoons (30 ml) orange juice

Canola oil as needed

½ cup (112 g) butter, melted

2 medium apples, peeled and diced (hold
    in water with a splash of cider vinegar
    to prevent discoloration)

2 bunches spinach, cleaned, stemmed, and
    coarsely chopped

Clean quails inside and out with a damp towel. Season inside and out with salt, pepper, and fresh thyme. In a bowl, combine cooked brown rice, apricots, bacon, and orange juice. Fill each quail with equal amounts of stuffing. Cut a small slit in one leg and place the other leg through it to prevent the bird from spreading out, or tie legs together with butcher's twine.

Heat grill to medium. Brush quail with small amount of canola oil and grill until done, approximately 20 to 25 minutes, rotating and basting with a small amount of melted butter until skin is golden brown. Be careful that birds do not get too dark.

Drain apples thoroughly and pat dry with paper towels. Heat remaining melted butter in a skillet and sauté apples for about 3 minutes, then add spinach and cook until just wilted. Season with salt and pepper.

To serve, place spinach and apple mixture in center of plate and place quail on top.

Wine pairing: Syrah

The Resort at Paws Up, Greenough, Montana

THE RESORT AT PAWS UP,
Greenough, Montana

Overnight Caramelized French Toast Casserole

serves six to eight

¼ pound (113 g) butter

¾ cup (175 ml) corn syrup

¾ cup (165 g) brown sugar

1 teaspoon (5 ml) vanilla extract

4 to 5 cups (170 to 224 g) day-old bread or rolls that have been torn into bite-sized chunks

8 eggs

1½ cups (355 ml) milk

1 tablespoon (3 g) cinnamon

2 tablespoons (12 g) granulated sugar

½ cup (60 g) roughly chopped walnuts or pecans

In a medium saucepan set over medium heat, combine butter, corn syrup, brown sugar, and vanilla extract. Heat while stirring until sugar dissolves. Pour mixture into a greased oven-proof 9 x 13-inch (23 x 33 cm) baking dish. Arrange bread chunks on top.

In another bowl, beat eggs and milk. Pour over bread chunks. Combine cinnamon, sugar, and chopped nuts; sprinkle over the top. Cover and refrigerate overnight.

In the morning, preheat oven to 375°F (190°F). Uncover the pan and bake for 30 to 40 minutes or until eggs set. Serve hot.

Rio Piedra Plantation, Camilla, Georgia

RIO PIEDRA PLANTATION, Camilla, Georgia

Fried Quail

serves two

2 whole quail
Water to cover quail
Peanut oil for deep-frying
1 cup (125 g) flour
1 teaspoon (2 g) celery salt
1 teaspoon (2 g) paprika
1 teaspoon (2 g) curry powder
½ teaspoon (1 g) ground white pepper
1 teaspoon (2 g) Old Bay or other
   seasoning mix

Soak quail in water for at least 1 hour. Remove and pat dry.

In a large heavy pot with deep sides, pour in peanut oil to a depth of 4 inches (10 cm). Heat peanut oil to 350°F (180°C) or until a piece of bread thrown into the oil begins to fry after a second or two.

Combine flour with remaining ingredients. Dredge quail in seasoned flour, covering it completely. Fry quail in hot oil until it floats. Let it float for about 1 minute, turning it over a couple of times in the oil. Remove from pot and drain on paper towel or newspaper.

Rio Piedra Plantation, Camilla, Georgia

Where's It From and What's It Taste Like?

Called bobwhite, partridge, and quail (blue, California, mountain, and Montezuma), these American quail are not related to the partridge family of bird in Europe. The meat is dark but mild. Since they're so small, they are usually served whole.

Quail Simmered in Mushroom Sauce

serves two

Salt and pepper
1 teaspoon (2 g) paprika
1 teaspoon (2 g) curry powder
1 teaspoon (2 g) celery salt
1 teaspoon (2 g) dried thyme
2 whole quail
Flour for dusting
1 tablespoon (15 ml) cooking oil
4 slices smoked bacon, cut into ½- inch
    (1.25 cm) strips
1 onion, chopped
1 clove garlic, minced
½ cup (86 g) chopped wild mushrooms
    (portobello, shiitake, or oyster
    mushrooms)
¼ cup (60 ml) brandy
½ cup (120 ml) red wine

Preheat oven to 350°F (180°C). Combine salt, pepper, paprika, curry powder, celery salt, and thyme. Season quail with mixture, then lightly dust in flour.

Heat oil in a frying pan until barely smoking. Brown quail on all sides in hot skillet. Set birds upright on a dish and set aside.

Discard oil in skillet. Add bacon strips and cook until slightly brown. Add onion and garlic and sauté until golden. Add mushrooms and let brown for a few minutes.

Take the pan off the burner and add brandy. Ignite with a match or lighter. When flames subside, return to burner and, using a wooden spoon, scrape up any brown bits sticking to the bottom of the pan. Add red wine and boil for 1 minute.

Pour sauce over birds, cover tightly with aluminum foil, and bake in oven for 1½ to 2 hours.

Rio Piedra Plantation, Camilla, Georgia

Duck and Black Bean Chili

serves six to eight

¼ cup (60 ml) vegetable oil

2 pounds (0.9 kg) skinless duck thigh or
    breast, diced

1 tablespoon (8 g) chopped garlic

1 onion, diced

½ cup (75 g) diced red bell pepper

½ cup (75 g) diced poblano pepper

½ cup (75 g) diced yellow bell pepper

1 cup Ancho Chili Purée (recipe follows)

1 tablespoon (6 g) toasted whole cumin

1 (14-ounce/400 g) can black beans,
    rinsed and drained

3 cups (700 ml) duck stock or chicken stock

Kosher salt to taste

Masa harina (or finely ground cornmeal)
    for thickening, as needed

Ancho Chili Purée

3 to 4 ancho chilies

4½ cups (1.1 liters) hot water, divided

Heat oil in large pot. Add duck and sear until golden brown. Add garlic, onion, peppers, ancho chili purée, cumin, black beans, and stock. Season with salt and simmer for 15 minutes. Add masa harina a few tablespoons at a time and cook for a few minutes after each addition. Repeat until the chili reaches preferred thickness.

For Ancho Chili Purée, place chilies in 4 cups (1 liter) hot water. Soak for 10 minutes. Remove chilies and discard soaking water. Place in blender with ½ cup (120 ml) fresh hot water and purée until smooth.

*Chef Gerard Thompson, Rough Creek Lodge & Resort,
Glen Rose, Texas*

ROUGH CREEK LODGE AND RESORT,
Glen Rose, Texas

BBQ Duck Tostada

serves to six

Duck Confit

⅛ cup (5 g) chopped herbs (thyme,
   rosemary, oregano)

⅛ cup (6 g) coarsely ground black pepper

½ cup (145 g) kosher salt

2 to 3 duck legs (leave fat on)

4 cups (1 liter) bacon or duck fat

½ carrot

½ onion

2 cloves garlic

Salsa

8 tomatillos, paper removed and washed

1 jalapeño

1 small yellow onion, chopped

1 cup (16 g) chopped cilantro

Salt and pepper to taste

Tortillas

1 cup (160 g) masa harina (or finely
   ground cornmeal)

¼ cup (31 g) flour

1 tablespoon (14 g) baking powder

¾ to 1 cup (176 to 235 ml) hot water

¼ cup (10 g) mixed chopped herbs (thyme,
   Italian parsley, and/or rosemary)

1 teaspoon (2 g) lemon zest

1 tablespoon (6 g) whole toasted cumin

Ancho Chili Glaze

5 ancho chilies

3 to 4 cups (700 ml to 1 liter) warm water

1 tablespoon (6 g) orange zest

1 tablespoon (15 ml) honey

Water for thinning glaze

Mix chopped herbs and pepper in medium bowl. Put salt in another medium bowl. Rinse duck in cold water. Toss each leg separately in bowl with pepper and herb mix. Then toss each in salt. Place on wire rack and refrigerate for 24 hours.

Place bacon or duck fat, carrot, onion, and garlic in heavy pot and heat to 190°F (88°C). Add duck and cook until duck falls from bone, about 2 hours. Do not let fat exceed 190°F (88°C). Remove duck from fat and cool. When cool, pick meat from bones and refrigerate. Discard bones.

For salsa, fill a small saucepan halfway with water. Add tomatillos, jalapeño, and onion. Bring to a simmer and cook until tomatillos are soft, about 7 or 8 minutes. Drain and cool vegetables. When cool, chop roughly and mix with cilantro. Season with salt and pepper. Set aside until ready to serve.

Combine all tortilla ingredients and knead to form a ball. If necessary, add more water until the dough is pliable. Shape dough into golf ball–sized balls. Roll out each ball between two pieces of waxed paper to form a 3½-inch (7.6 cm) tortilla.

To make Ancho Chili Glaze, preheat oven to 350°F (180°C). Toast chilies in oven for 30 seconds. Soak chilies in warm water for 20 minutes, then remove seeds and stems (no need to peel). Blend chilies, orange zest, and honey in blender. Add water to thin, if needed. Set aside and keep warm.

Cook each tortilla in an ungreased skillet for 30 seconds; turn tortilla and continue cooking for 1 minute. Keep warm.

To serve: Add the duck to the Ancho Chili Glaze and warm. Place tomatillo salsa on plate, creating a circle. Put tortilla in center of plate and top with duck mixture. Garnish with lettuce, cheese, cilantro, and tomatoes, if desired.

*Chef Gerard Thompson, Rough Creek Lodge & Resort,
Glen Rose, Texas*

Duck Salad

serves four

Marinade for duck

1 cup (235 ml) vegetable oil
¼ cup (60 ml) balsamic vinegar
1 teaspoon (5 ml) honey
1 teaspoon (0.8 g) fresh thyme
1 shallot, minced
1 teaspoon (2 g) coarsely ground black
  pepper
2 whole (8-ounce/225 g) skinless duck
  breasts

Vinaigrette for Salad

1 cup (235 ml) olive oil
⅓ cup (78 ml) balsamic vinegar
2 teaspoons (7 g) chopped shallots
1 teaspoon (2 g) orange zest
Kosher salt and coarsely ground black
  pepper to taste

Salad

½ pound (225 g) mixed baby greens
¼ cup (25 g) walnut halves
¼ cup (30 g) assorted dried berries
  (cranberries, cherries, blueberries)
¼ cup (37 g) crumbled blue cheese

Mix vegetable oil, balsamic vinegar, honey, thyme, shallot, and pepper to make marinade. Add duck and marinate for at least 4 hours. Light wood or charcoal grill and wait until flames subside and coals are covered by white ash. Grill duck breasts for a few minutes on each side, or until golden brown and cooked through. Let rest for 10 minutes. Cut duck into thin strips.

Combine all vinaigrette ingredients. Unused portion may be stored covered tightly and refrigerated for up to 2 weeks.

Place greens, walnuts, berries, and blue cheese in a large salad bowl and toss with ¼ cup (60 ml) vinaigrette.

To serve, divide salad equally among 4 chilled plates. Divide duck and place on top of salad on each plate.

Chef Gerard Thompson, Rough Creek Lodge & Resort, Glen Rose, Texas

Game Bird Pot-au-Feu

serves four

Marinade
1 cup (235 ml) vegetable oil
1 clove fresh garlic, crushed
1 tablespoon (15 ml) sherry wine vinegar
2 tablespoons (12 g) lemon zest
1 tablespoon (2.5 g) fresh thyme, chopped
Kosher salt
Cracked black pepper

Game Bird
2 whole fresh dove (or squab)
1 whole (2½- to 3-pound/1.1 to 1.4 kg)
*   fresh pheasant*
2 boneless quail, cut in half
Marinade (recipe above)
1 gallon (3.8 liters) water
2 plum tomatoes, quartered
1 onion, roughly chopped
1 carrot, roughly chopped
1 clove garlic, finely chopped
4 sprigs fresh thyme
1 bay leaf
2 cups (470 ml) Pinot Noir
8 tablespoons (1 stick/112 g) unsalted
*   butter, cut in small pieces*
4 ounces (113 g) foie gras, cut in small
*   pieces (substitute 2 ounces/56 g chicken*
*   liver and 2 ounces/56 g butter if foie*
*   gras is not available)*
2 tablespoons (30 ml) vegetable oil
1 pound duck sausage, cut into 2-inch
*   (5 cm) pieces*

Combine all marinade ingredients in blender and run for 2 minutes.

Bone dove and pheasant, separating breasts, leg, and thigh from carcass. Separate pheasant legs from thighs. Place dove breasts, pheasant breasts, pheasant thighs, and quail in deep dish; pour marinade over meat and marinate 4 hours. Do not marinate duck sausage.

Preheat oven to 375°F (190°C). Place pheasant and dove carcass, along with dove legs and thighs and pheasant legs, in large roasting pan and roast until golden brown. Remove from oven. Transfer to stockpot with water, tomatoes, onion, carrot, garlic, thyme, and bay leaf. Simmer 3 hours. Strain broth and discard bones.

Pour Pinot Noir in a large stainless steel saucepan and reduce on medium-high heat until syrupy and about 1 tablespoon (15 ml) remains. Add bird broth and reduce until 2 cups (470 ml) remain. Place broth in blender (while hot) and add butter pieces until all are incorporated. Add foie gras and continue blending until incorporated. Reserve and keep warm.

Remove the dove (or squab) breasts, quail, and pheasant breasts and thighs from marinade. Heat oil in a large (12-inch/30 cm) frying pan. Place pheasant breasts and thighs in hot pan along with duck sausage. Brown all over and remove. Place on baking sheet and bake in oven until cooked through. Reheat the frying pan on high heat. Add quail and dove to hot frying pan and cook until slightly pink in center.

To serve, place 1 pheasant thigh, 1 dove breast, ½ quail, ½ pheasant breast, and ¼ of the duck sausage on each plate. Cover with warm sauce and serve.

Chef Gerard Thompson, Rough Creek Lodge & Resort, Glen Rose, Texas

Grilled Romaine with Sun-Dried Tomato-Caper Relish

serves four

Romaine

2 small heads romaine

1 lemon

2 tablespoons (30 ml) olive oil

Salt and coarsely ground black pepper

Sun-Dried Tomato-Caper Relish

2 ripe red tomatoes, seeded and diced

¼ cup (14 g) diced sun-dried tomatoes

*4 cloves garlic, roasted in 350°F (180°C)
    oven for 30 minutes*

*2 tablespoons (17 g) capers, drained and
    rinsed*

*¼ cup (34 g) kalamata olives, pitted and
    chopped*

1 tablespoon (2.6 g) thinly sliced fresh basil

Romano Cheese Dressing

1 clove garlic, minced

1 egg

2 ounces (57 g) drained anchovy fillets

1 teaspoon (5 ml) Dijon mustard

Juice of 1 lemon

*2 tablespoons (30 ml) red wine vinegar,
    more as needed*

½ cup (120 ml) olive oil

½ cup (120 ml) vegetable oil

½ cup (66 g) finely grated Romano cheese

Cracked black pepper

Dash Worcestershire sauce

Preheat grill to medium-high. Split romaine heads in half from the stem to the top. Brush with lemon and olive oil. Season with salt and pepper. Grill on all sides until slightly charred. Remove from grill and cool.

Combine all relish ingredients and refrigerate until ready to serve.

In a food processor, combine garlic, egg, anchovies, Dijon mustard, lemon juice, and red wine vinegar and blend until smooth. Slowly add oils. If dressing gets too thick, it can be thinned with a little more red wine vinegar. Blend in Romano cheese. Season with cracked black pepper and Worcestershire sauce. Leftover dressing can be refrigerated for two weeks.

To serve, place one piece grilled romaine lettuce on each salad plate. Spoon some Sun-Dried Tomato-Caper Relish around romaine on plate. Drizzle a generous amount of Romano Cheese Dressing all over the romaine and relish.

**Chef Gerard Thompson, Rough Creek Lodge & Resort,
Glen Rose, Texas**

Pheasant Pot Stickers with Mango Sauce

makes fourteen to sixteen two-bite appetizers

4 ounces (113 g) raw pheasant, finely
    chopped

2 ounces (66 g) raw, fresh foie gras, diced
    (or 1 ounce/28 g chicken liver plus 2
    tablespoons/28 g butter)

½ cup (35 g) lobster mushrooms, finely
    chopped and cooked

1 teaspoon (3 g) finely chopped garlic

1 teaspoon (2 g) grated ginger

1 teaspoon (5 ml) sesame oil

1 egg

1 tablespoon (15 ml) water

1 package gyoza skins (or use wonton
    wrappers cut into rounds with a cookie
    cutter)

8 cups (2 liters) salted water

2 tablespoons (30 ml) vegetable oil for
    cooking

Mango sauce

1 small shallot, minced

¼ cup (60 ml) chili garlic sauce (available
    at most Asian supermarkets)

½ teaspoon (1 g) freshly ground black
    pepper

¼ cup (60 ml) soy sauce

½ cup (120 ml) rice wine vinegar

½ tablespoon (0.5 g) chopped fresh
    cilantro

1 cup (235 ml) mango purée

Kosher salt to taste

Mix pheasant, foie gras, mushrooms, garlic, ginger, and sesame oil together. In a separate bowl, whisk egg and 1 tablespoon (15 ml) water. Lay gyoza skins out 2 at a time. Brush lightly with egg mixture. Place 1 tablespoon (13 g) pheasant mixture in center of each gyoza skin and fold over into half-moon shape. Press edges to seal. Cook pot stickers in gently boiling salted water for 3 to 4 minutes. Drain on paper towels. Preheat a nonstick frying pan, add oil, and sear drained pot stickers until golden brown.

Combine all sauce ingredients and mix well. Serve with pot stickers.

Chef Gerard Thompson, Rough Creek Lodge & Resort, Glen Rose, Texas

Roast Pheasant

serves six

1 tablespoon (15 ml) balsamic vinegar
1 clove garlic, minced
1 tablespoon (1 g) chopped rosemary
1 teaspoon (5 ml) honey
1 shallot, minced
1 tablespoon (15 ml) orange juice
1 cup (235 ml) vegetable oil
6 whole (6- to 8-ounce/170 to 225 g)
   pheasant breasts

Mix balsamic vinegar, garlic, rosemary, honey, shallot, orange juice, and vegetable oil to make marinade. Marinate pheasant breasts for 4 hours.

Preheat oven to 350°F (180°C). Remove pheasant breasts from marinade and pat dry. Heat frying pan on high and sear pheasant breasts. Transfer to baking sheet and bake in oven for 12 to 15 minutes. (Pheasant breasts can also be cooked over an open fire.)

Chef Gerard Thompson, Rough Creek Lodge & Resort, Glen Rose, Texas

Where's It From and What's It Taste Like?

From Asia, the female pheasant, weighing in at about 3 pounds (1.4 kg), is the better choice for the table. Its meat is more tender, plump, and juicy than that of the male (which comes in at 5 pounds [2.3 kg]). Farm-raised pheasant tastes less gamey than wild; it tastes similar to chicken.

Roast Venison Steak with Fall Vegetable Ratatouille

serves six

Venison

1 tablespoon (15 ml) balsamic vinegar

1 clove garlic, finely chopped

1 tablespoon (2 g) chopped rosemary

1 teaspoon (5 ml) honey

1 shallot, finely chopped

1 tablespoon (15 ml) orange juice

1 cup (235 ml) plus 1 tablespoon (15 ml)
vegetable oil

6 (5- to 6-ounce/142 to 170 g) venison
loin steaks

Ratatouille

2 tablespoons (28 g) soft butter

1 tablespoon (9 g) chopped fresh garlic

½ cup (80 g) chopped red onion

1 cup (140 g) finely chopped butternut
squash

1 cup (140 g) finely chopped acorn squash

1 cup (86 g) finely chopped portobello
mushroom

1 tablespoon (2 g) fresh thyme, chopped

Kosher salt and freshly cracked pepper
to taste

In a large bowl combine vinegar, garlic, rosemary, honey, shallot, orange juice, and 1 cup (235 ml) vegetable oil. Mix well. Add venison and turn over in mixture to cover well. Cover and refrigerate for 4 hours.

Preheat oven to 350°F (180°C). Remove venison from marinade and pat dry. Heat 1 tablespoon (15 ml) oil in a frying pan until barely smoking. Add venison steaks and sear each side until golden brown. Transfer to oven for 8 to 10 minutes or until medium-rare. (Steaks can also be grilled over an open fire.)

Heat a frying pan set on medium-high; melt butter and sauté garlic and onion until the onion softens. Add squash and continue cooking 3 to 5 minutes until squash is fork-tender. Add portabella mushrooms and thyme. Cook 3 minutes longer, stirring occasionally. Season with salt and pepper.

To serve, divide ratatouille among six plates and place a venison steak alongside.

Chef Gerard Thompson, Rough Creek Lodge & Resort,
Glen Rose, Texas

Sherry-Maple Glazed Wild Game Bird Caesar Salad

serves four

Quail

Zest of ½ lemon
1 teaspoon (1 g) chopped thyme
1 teaspoon (3 g) chopped fresh garlic
½ cup (120 ml) vegetable oil
1 tablespoon (15 ml) balsamic vinegar
1 boneless quail

Pheasant

2 fresh pheasants
4 cups (1 liter) orange juice
½ cup (120 ml) rice wine vinegar
½ cup (120 ml) apple cider vinegar
¼ cup (55 g) brown sugar
2 cloves garlic, chopped
½ onion, chopped
1 sprig thyme
1 sprig rosemary
1 ancho chili, seeded
¼ cup (73 g) kosher salt

Sherry-Maple Glaze

½ cup (120 ml) sherry vinegar
½ cup (120 ml) maple syrup

Mix lemon zest, thyme, garlic, oil, and vinegar; pour over quail, cover, and refrigerate for 4 hours. Grill quail over charcoal for 3 to 5 minutes on each side or until medium-well but still pink in the center.

Put pheasants in a large pot. In another saucepan, bring next 10 ingredients (orange juice through kosher salt) to a boil; cool and pour over pheasants. Cover and refrigerate 4 hours. Preheat grill to medium high. Grill pheasant for 5 to 8 minutes on each side, until well browned and crispy. Let rest for 5 minutes before slicing.

Combine vinegar and syrup in a small saucepan and cook until reduced to syrupy consistency. Keep warm until ready to use.

Caesar Dressing

⅛ cup (30 ml) sherry wine vinegar

⅛ cup (30 ml) fresh lemon juice

2 cloves garlic, finely chopped

1 tablespoon (15 ml) Dijon mustard

2 teaspoons (10 ml) Worcestershire sauce

8 anchovy fillets, minced

3 egg yolks

1 cup (235 ml) olive oil

Salt and pepper to taste

¾ cup (85 g) grated Romano cheese,
    divided

Grilled Romaine Lettuce

1 large head romaine lettuce, quartered

1 tablespoon (15 ml) olive oil

Juice of 1 lemon

Salt and pepper

In a medium bowl, combine vinegar, lemon juice, garlic, Dijon mustard, Worcestershire sauce, anchovies, and egg yolks and whisk until frothy. Continue to whisk while slowly adding olive oil. Season with salt and pepper. Fold in ½ cup (66 g) Romano cheese and save the other ¼ cup (19 g) for finishing the dish. Cover and refrigerate dressing until ready to serve.

Drizzle lettuce with oil and lemon juice, season with salt and pepper. Grill over hot charcoal.

To serve, spoon 3 or 4 tablespoons (45 or 60 ml) Caesar Dressing on plate. Place hot grilled romaine wedge in center of plate and top with grilled quail and pheasant. Drizzle with Sherry-Maple Glaze and sprinkle with remaining Romano cheese.

Chef Gerard Thompson, Rough Creek Lodge & Resort, Glen Rose, Texas

Sherry-Maple Glazed Quail

serves two to four

Quail
Zest of ½ lemon
1 teaspoon (0.3 g) chopped thyme
1 teaspoon (3 g) minced fresh garlic
½ cup (120 ml) vegetable oil
1 tablespoon (15 ml) balsamic vinegar
4 whole fresh quail
1 tablespoon (8 g) chili powder

Sherry-Maple Glaze
½ cup (120 ml) sherry vinegar
½ cup (120 ml) maple syrup
¼ cup (60 ml) grainy mustard

Combine lemon zest, thyme, garlic, oil, and vinegar. Pour over quail and marinate in the refrigerator for 1 hour.

Light charcoal grill and wait until coals are covered with white ash. Remove quail from marinade and season with chili powder. Grill quail over charcoal for 3 to 5 minutes on each side or until medium-well but still pink in the center.

Place glaze ingredients in a stainless steel saucepan. Reduce to a syrup, then spoon over grilled quail.

Chef Gerard Thompson, Rough Creek Lodge & Resort, Glen Rose, Texas

Game Tips

■ *Of all the game birds, quail is said to be the sweetest and most tender. Weighing in at 4 to 8 ounces (113 to 227 g) each, one bird makes one entrée. They're so tasty that there is no need to overdo seasonings.*

Smithfield Ham Biscuits

makes about eight to ten biscuits

2 cups (275 g) flour
2 teaspoons (9 g) baking powder
½ teaspoon (2.5 g) baking soda
½ teaspoon (2.5 g) salt
1 teaspoon (5 g) cracked black pepper
1 tablespoon (4 g) sugar
6 tablespoons (85 g) cold butter
⅔ cup (160 ml) buttermilk
1 cup (235 ml) chopped Smithfield ham
½ cup (120 ml) chopped scallions

Preheat oven to 375°F (190°C). Place flour, baking powder, baking soda, salt, pepper, sugar, and butter into the bowl of a food processor and pulse until butter is chopped into pea-sized pieces. Add buttermilk, ham, and scallions. Pulse just a few times until ingredients are barely incorporated. On a lightly floured surface, roll out to 1-inch-thick (2.5 cm) slab and cut into desired shape. Transfer to baking sheet and bake in oven for 12 to 15 minutes, until golden brown on top.

Chef Gerard Thompson, Rough Creek Lodge & Resort, Glen Rose, Texas

Surf & Turf (Venison and Maine Lobster)

serves four

8 cups (2 liters) plus 1 tablespoon (15 ml)
   vegetable oil , divided

1 pound (450 g) venison loin, cut into 4
   equal pieces

1 (12-ounce/340 g) package tempura
   batter mix

2 (1-pound/450 g) Maine lobsters, cooked,
   shelled, and tail split in half

2 pounds (0.9 kg) fresh spinach

2 teaspoons (6 g) chopped garlic

Sauce

1 red bell pepper, peeled and seeded

8 cups (2 liters) veal or beef stock, reduced
   to 1½ cups (355 ml)

Kosher salt to taste

Cracked black pepper to taste

Heat 1 tablespoon (15 ml) vegetable oil in a large skillet set on high. Add venison to pan; sear on both sides and cook until medium-rare. Transfer to a plate and keep warm until ready to serve.

Heat 8 cups (2 liters) vegetable oil in large skillet over medium heat to 350°F (180°C), or until a piece of bread dropped in the oil begins to fry after a second or two. Follow manufacturer's instructions for preparing tempura batter. Dip lobster tails into tempura batter and fry for 3 minutes. Remove and drain on paper towels.

In a nonstick saucepan over medium heat, sauté spinach with garlic and divide among four warm plates. Pour sauce over venison and lobster.

Combine all ingredients in a blender or food processor. Blend until smooth. Transfer to a small sauce pan and simmer for 5 minutes. Season to taste.

To serve, divide spinach among four warmed dinner plates. Top with venison and crisp lobster tail. Spoon some sauce on and around the lobster and venison and serve.

**Chef Gerard Thompson, Rough Creek Lodge & Resort,
Glen Rose, Texas**

Warm Fingerling Potato Salad

serves four

1 medium-sized beet

2 tablespoons (30 ml) olive oil, divided

Salt and pepper

12 fingerling potatoes

1 teaspoon (1 g) dried thyme

4 ounces (113 g) cooked thin green beans
   (about 12 pieces)

Vinaigrette

1 teaspoon (5 ml) Dijon mustard

1 shallot, thinly sliced

1 tablespoon (15 ml) sherry wine vinegar

3 tablespoons (45 ml) olive oil

Preheat oven to 400°F (200°C). Place beet on roasting pan. Drizzle with 1 tablespoon (15 ml) olive oil and season with salt and pepper. Cover with aluminum foil. Roast until tender when pierced with tip of knife (about 1 hour). Remove from oven and let sit covered until cool to the touch. Peel skin and discard. Cut beet into thin wedges.

Place fingerling potatoes on another roasting pan; drizzle with remaining olive oil, thyme, salt, and pepper. Roast potatoes 10-15 minutes until tender. Let cool and then slice potatoes in half lengthwise. Toss potatoes, beets, and green beans together. Add vinaigrette and season with salt and pepper. Divide among 4 plates and serve.

Combine mustard, shallots, and vinegar. Slowly whisk in olive oil.

Chef Gerard Thompson, Rough Creek Lodge & Resort, Glen Rose, Texas

Wild Mushroom and Sweet Garlic Bread Pudding

serves six

3 tablespoons (42 g) butter, plus more for
  greasing pan
1 shallot, finely diced
2 cups (144 g) chopped assorted fresh
  wild mushrooms (morel, porcini, or
  chanterelle)
1 tablespoon (2 g) chopped assorted herbs
  (thyme, rosemary, oregano, or flat-leaf
  parsley)
1 cup (235 ml) heavy cream
2 large eggs
1 loaf (10 ounces/284 g) ourdough bread,
  diced into 4 cups
½ cup (68 g) roasted garlic, chopped
Salt and freshly ground black pepper

Preheat oven to 350°F (180°C). In a frying pan, melt butter over medium-high heat. Add shallot and mushrooms. Cook for 3-5 minutes or until mushrooms are cooked through. Add herbs and cool. In a stainless steel bowl, mix heavy cream and eggs. Add bread, cooked mushrooms, and roasted garlic. Season with salt and pepper to taste. Butter a large 6-cup muffin tin and divide mixture among cups. Bake in oven for 20 to 25 minutes or until golden brown and a knife inserted into the center of 1 cup comes out clean. Remove from oven and serve with your favorite meat, game, or poultry.

*Chef Gerard Thompson, Rough Creek Lodge & Resort,
Glen Rose, Texas*

Venison and Sweet Potato Hash

serves four to six

4 to 5 cups (1 to 1.2 liters) salted water
1 Idaho potato, diced
1 sweet potato, diced
¼ cup (60 ml) vegetable oil
Salt and pepper to taste
1 cup corn, sliced from a cob
1 small red bell pepper, diced
1 small yellow bell pepper, diced
2 cups (470 ml) diced venison meat
1 bunch green onions, chopped

Bring salted water to a simmer in a large pot and add Idaho and sweet potatoes. When potatoes are cooked, plunge them into ice water to stop the cooking. Drain and dry the potatoes.

Heat vegetable oil in a large frying pan set on high. Add cooked Idaho and sweet potatoes to sauté until golden brown. Season with salt and pepper and continue to cook. Add corn and peppers and sauté for another minute. Transfer cooked vegetables to a bowl and keep warm until ready to serve. Add venison meat to hot pan and sauté, stirring occasionally, until meat is fully cooked and tender, about 20 minutes. Remove from heat and toss in green onions. Add vegetables and stir gently to combine. Taste and adjust seasonings as desired.

Serving suggestion: Serve with poached or fried eggs on top with some hot red pepper sauce.

Chef Gerard Thompson, Rough Creek Lodge & Resort, Glen Rose, Texas

Sweet Onion Risotto

serves six

4 to 5 cups (0.9 to 1 l) chicken broth

1 stick (4 ounces/112 g) salted butter,
    divided

1 medium onion, finely chopped

2 cups (400 g) Italian Arborio rice

½ cup (120 ml) white wine

1 tablespoon lemon zest

½ cup (50 g) grated Parmigiano-
    Reggiano cheese

Kosher salt

Coarsely ground black pepper

Heat the chicken broth to a simmer and keep hot. In a separate heavy-bottomed pot set on medium-low heat, melt ½ stick (2 ounces/56 g) butter. Add onion and cook slowly for 12 to 18 minutes, or until golden brown. Stir frequently to be sure onion caramelizes and does not burn. Add rice and stir with wooden spoon while cooking for 2 minutes. Add wine and cook until wine is absorbed. Turn heat up to medium-high. Add hot chicken broth 1 cup (235 ml) at a time. Stir constantly while cooking. Let rice absorb each cup of broth before adding the next. When the rice develops a creamy consistency like oatmeal and a has a slight crunch when bitten (about 15 to 20 minutes), stop adding broth and stir in remaining ½ stick (2 ounces/56g) butter, lemon zest, and cheese. Season with salt and pepper and serve.

This is a nice accompaniment to roast pheasant.

*Chef Gerard Thompson, Rough Creek Lodge & Resort,
Glen Rose, Texas*

Valrhona Chocolate Buttermilk Cake

serves eight

1 cup (200 g) granulated sugar

¾ cup (94 g) flour

½ cup (43 g) Valrhona cocoa powder (or
   other high-quality cocoa)

1 teaspoon (5 g) baking soda

½ teaspoon (2 g) baking powder

¼ teaspoon (1.5 g) salt

½ cup (120 ml) brewed coffee, cooled

½ cup (120 ml) buttermilk

4 tablespoons (56 g) butter, melted

2 eggs

1 teaspoon (5 ml) vanilla

Shortening or additional soft butter for
   greasing pan

Preheat oven to 350°F (180°C). In a large bowl, sift together sugar, flour, cocoa, baking soda, baking powder, and salt. Set aside. In another bowl, whisk together coffee, buttermilk, butter, eggs, and vanilla. Whisk dry ingredients into wet until well combined. Generously grease 10-inch (25 cm) round cake pan. Pour in batter*. Bake for about 50 minutes or until toothpick comes out clean. Cool thoroughly. Run a knife around the edge of the pan to loosen the cake. Invert onto a plate and lift pan away from cake. Serve with berries, chocolate sauce, or ice cream, if desired.

* Since top may rise too high and overflow, put small baking sheet underneath in the oven to catch any runover.

*Chef Gerard Thompson, Rough Creek Lodge & Resort,
Glen Rose, Texas*

Warm Pear & Cranberry Tart

makes four individual tarts

Tart Dough

1½ cups (188 g) flour

1 teaspoon (6 g)kosher salt

1 teaspoon (4 g)sugar

1 stick (4 ounces/112 g) cold butter

⅓ to ½ cup (80 to 120 ml) cold water

1 egg, lightly whisked

Filling

2 cups (300 g) peeled, cored, and diced
ripe pears

1 cup (95 g) fresh cranberries

1 vanilla bean, split and scraped (or
substitute 1 tablespoon/15 ml vanilla
extract)

½ cup (100 g) granulated sugar, plus
some for sprinkling

½ stick (2 ounces/56 g) cold butter, cut
into small dice

2 tablespoons (15 g) flour

½ cup (63 g) slivered almonds

In food processor, combine flour, salt, and sugar. Pulse mixture, gradually adding butter in small chunks. Continue pulsing until butter forms pea-sized pieces and the mixture appears gravelly. Slowly add cold water while pulsing. Stop just as dough begins to stick together. It should still appear very rough-textured. Do not overmix. Shape into a ball and flatten into a disk 1 inch (2.5 cm) thick. Wrap dough tightly in plastic and chill in the refrigerator until firm, about 1 hour. When ready to use, divide dough into four equal portions. Shape each portion into a ball and press or roll out into 5-inch (12.5 cm) disks.

Preheat oven to 375°F (190°C). Toss all filling ingredients together except almonds. Lay pastry disks on a lightly greased cookie sheet. Place some fruit mixture in the center of each pastry disk. Carefully fold sides of dough up and toward the center, overlapping and crimping as you go. When finished, there should be a small hole in center. Brush pastry with egg and sprinkle with sugar and slivered almonds. Bake for 20 to 25 minutes or until golden brown. Serve with your favorite ice cream.

Chef Gerard Thompson, Rough Creek Lodge & Resort, Glen Rose, Texas

Peach and Pecan Cornmeal Buckle

serves six

½ pound (227 g) unsalted butter at room
   temperature

1 cup (200 g) granulated sugar, divided

2 cups (250 g) flour, divided

½ cup (80 g) cornmeal

2 teaspoons (9 g) baking soda

1 cup (235 ml) buttermilk

½ cup (110 g) brown sugar

½ cup (112 g) unsalted butter, cold

½ cup (50 g) pecans

Shortening or soft butter for greasing pan

2 ripe peaches, stone removed and cut into
   12 slices each

Preheat oven to 350°F (180°C). In the bowl of an electric mixer, beat ½ pound (227 g) butter and ½ cup (100 g) sugar until fluffy and light yellow in color. In a separate bowl, combine 1 cup (125 g) flour, cornmeal, and baking soda. With the mixer running on low, add one third of the flour mixture to the butter mixture, then one third of the buttermilk, alternating until all is incorporated. Do not overmix.

In a food processor, combine remaining ½ cup (100 g) sugar, brown sugar, remaining 1 cup (125 g) flour, cold butter, and pecans. Pulse until barely mixed and still gravelly in texture.

Grease 9 x 13-inch (23 by 33 cm) pan with butter. Arrange peach slices in bottom of pan. Top with batter and sprinkle with pecan mixture. Bake 20 to 25 minutes or until golden brown and a knife inserted into the center comes out clean. Slice into six portions. Top with your favorite ice cream and serve warm.

*Chef Gerard Thompson, Rough Creek Lodge & Resort,
Glen Rose, Texas*

Bison Sirloin with Roasted Garlic Cream Sauce

serves four

2 pounds (0.9 kg) bison sirloin
1 tablespoon (15 ml) olive oil
Salt and pepper to taste
4 cloves garlic, minced
1 onion, chopped
1 stalk celery, chopped
1 cup (235 ml) Riesling wine
1 cup (235 ml) cream

Preheat oven to 350°F (180°C). Heat a heavy-bottomed roasting pan on the stovetop. Coat sirloin in oil, salt, and pepper and sear in hot roasting pan, turning to brown both sides. Transfer pan to oven and roast for 1 hour or until an instant-read thermometer registers an internal temperature of 140°F (60°C) for medium-rare. Transfer the roast to a cutting board and cover loosely with foil to keep warm until ready to serve.

Reheat the roasting pan on the stovetop and add garlic, onion, and celery; cook briefly, then add wine and cream. Reduce sauce for 2 to 3 minutes, strain (if desired), and spoon over sliced bison.

Chef John Noel Gilbertson, CEC, Spring Lake Hunting Lodge and Resort, Oldham, South Dakota

SPRING LAKE HUNTING LODGE AND RESORT, Oldham, South Dakota

Cheap Whiskey Sauce

serves twelve or more

4 cups (1 liter) cheap whiskey
½ pound (225 g) butter
1 pound (450 g) brown sugar
½ cup (60 g) chopped nuts
¼ cup (32 g) cornstarch, mixed with 1
    cup (235 ml) water

In a large, heavy-bottomed pan, combine whiskey, butter, brown sugar, and nuts and bring to a simmer. Keep a lid close by to throw onto the pan should it flame up. After cooking for about 15 minutes, slowly blend in cornstarch mixture and cook for several more minutes until glossy and syrupy in texture.

Serve over baked or sautéed boneless pheasant, chicken, or duck. Keep leftover sauce covered in refrigerator for up to 2 weeks.

Chef John Noel Gilbertson, CEC, Spring Lake Hunting Lodge and Resort, Oldham, South Dakota

Game Tips

- Buffalo is high in protein and has 30 percent less cholesterol than beef. With little fat, it cooks up quickly and tastes best if it is cooked rare to medium-rare. When grilling steaks, keep them 6 inches (15 cm) from the heat and baste them so they don't dry out. Buffalo can replace beef in any recipe.
- Bacteria can multiply if meat is not kept cold enough. Danger-zone temperatures for meat are 40°–140°F (4°–60°C).

Dakota Pheasant Supreme

serves four

4 whole pheasant breasts

½ cup (120 ml) Merlot, divided

½ teaspoon (3 g) salt

½ cup (120 ml) veal or beef stock

1 (8-ounce/225 g) package wild
    rice blend, prepared according to
    manufacturer's directions

Preheat oven to 375°F. Purée 2 pheasant breasts in food processor for 30 seconds or until smooth. Add ¼ cup (60 ml) wine and salt and pulse a few times until blended.

Line a baking sheet with parchment paper. Coat remaining 2 pheasant breasts with the pheasant mixture and place them on the parchment paper. Bake in oven for 25 to 30 minutes, or until an instant read thermometer placed in the center of a breast registers 145°F (63°C). Remove pan from oven. Transfer pheasant breasts to a cutting board and cover loosely with foil to keep warm.

Place roasting pan on stovetop burner set on medium-high. Add remaining wine and reduce by half. Add stock and reduce until the mixture sizzles.

To serve, spoon the wild rice onto a warm platter. Slice each pheasant breast through the middle on the bias. Place the slices on top of wild rice and drizzle some pan sauce over them.

Chef John Noel Gilbertson, CEC, Spring Lake Hunting Lodge and Resort, Oldham, South Dakota

Honey-Lime Barbeque Sauce

serves eight

1 cup (235 ml) honey (local honey is
    recommended)

½ cup (120 ml) vinegar (balsamic is
    recommended)

Juice of 2 limes

2 tablespoons (30 ml) soy sauce or tomato
    juice

1 tablespoon (8 g) cornstarch mixed with 2
    tablespoons (30 ml) cold water

In a small saucepan set over medium heat, cook the honey until golden brown. Add vinegar, lime juice, and soy sauce (or tomato juice). Bring to low simmer. Whisk in cornstarch mixture and simmer for several more minutes until thickened and translucent. Serve with all kinds of grilled meats, especially poultry. Store leftover sauce in refrigerator for up to a month.

Chef John Noel Gilbertson, CEC, Spring Lake Hunting Lodge and Resort, Oldham, South Dakota

Marchand de Vin (Sauce of the Wine Merchant)

serves four

2 cups (½ liter) red wine

1 shallot, minced

1 bouquet garni (thyme, parsley, and bay
   leaf bundled and wrapped tightly in
   cheesecloth)

6 whole black peppercorns

2 tablespoons (60 ml) heavy cream

¼ pound (112 g) unsalted butter

Salt to taste

Reduce wine, shallot, bouquet garni, and peppercorns by three-fourths so only ½ cup (118 ml) remains. Strain into saucepan (discard solids), add cream, and bring back to simmer. Take pan off the burner and add gradually add butter in small pieces while whisking rapidly to create a creamy sauce. If necessary, reheat very gently.

Season with salt to taste and serve immediately over grilled pheasant, quail, or other game meat.

Chef John Noel Gilbertson, CEC, Spring Lake Hunting Lodge and Resort, Oldham, South Dakota

Game Tips

- Cooked muscle meat is safe to eat if the internal temperature is 160°F (71°C) throughout. Whole game birds are safe cooked to 165°F (74°C) at the innermost part of the thigh and wing and at the thickest part of the breast.
- Game birds are considered white meat, but because they are birds of flight, the meat is darker than chicken.
- All terrestrial game animals are considered red meat.

Ringneck Pheasant "Rustica"

serves eight

2 pounds (0.9 kg) pheasant meat (breasts
    and thighs)
1 cup (125 g) flour, seasoned with salt and
    pepper
8 tablespoons (112 g) butter, divided
12 cloves garlic
1 large onion
4 cups (1 liter) merlot
4 cups (1 liter) veal or beef stock
1 sprig fresh thyme (optional)
Salt and pepper to taste
1 pound (450 g) mushrooms, quartered
1 pound (450 g) pearl onions

Preheat a large (12-inch/30 cm) frying pan.

Roll pheasant meat in seasoned flour. Heat 4 tablespoons (56 g) butter in pan until butter sizzles. Sauté pheasant. Do not crowd the pan. Sauté in batches if pan isn't big enough. Brown meat on both sides. Remove pieces from pan as they are browned.

When all the pheasant meat is cooked, add garlic, onion, and wine to pan. Bring to a simmer and add stock. Return all pheasant pieces to pan, cover, and let simmer. Add half a sprig of thyme, cover, and cook for 1½ hours.

In a separate pan, sauté mushrooms and pearl onions in remaining butter until brown and set aside.

Remove meat from stock and boil to reduce liquid by half. Add mushroom mixture and pheasant meat to liquid, heat, season with salt and pepper, and serve over wild rice or pasta.

Wine recommendation: California Merlot

Chef John Noel Gilbertson, CEC, Spring Lake Hunting Lodge and Resort, Oldham, South Dakota

Pretzel-Breaded Wild Turkey

serves two

1 cup (125 g) flour
4 eggs, beaten
1 cup (235 ml) chopped pretzels
1 pound (450 g) wild turkey breast, sliced
    about ¼-inch (6.3 mm) thick
1 tablespoon (15 ml) vegetable oil
Salt and pepper
1 tablespoon (14 g) butter
1 tablespoon (15 ml) honey

Put flour, eggs, and chopped pretzels in separate bowls. First coat the turkey slices in flour, then the egg, and finally the pretzels.

Heat oil and butter in 12-inch (30 cm) frying pan. Gently place breaded turkey slices in pan. Reduce heat to low. Cook about 2 minutes on each side, until golden brown.

Remove from pan, drain on paper towels, and season with salt and pepper. Garnish with thin streams of honey and serve immediately.

Chef John Noel Gilbertson, CEC, Spring Lake Hunting Lodge and Resort, Oldham, South Dakota

Smoked Pheasant Chowder

serves six to eight

1 smoked pheasant

1 large carrot, peeled and diced

1 large onion, peeled and diced

½ celery stalk, diced

1 tablespoon (9 g) minced garlic

1½ to 2 quarts (1.4 to 1.9 liters) water, or
  enough to cover bird

1 cup (160 g) uncooked wild rice

½ cup (63 g) flour

8 tablespoons (112 g) butter, softened

1 cup (164 g) frozen corn kernels

Salt and pepper

2 cups (470 ml) heavy cream

In a large pot, combine pheasant, carrot, onion, celery, garlic, and water and simmer for 2 to 3 hours.

Follow package directions for cooking wild rice. Remove pheasant from broth and cool. Pull meat from bones in bite-sized pieces and reserve.

Blend flour and butter together to form a thick paste. Return broth with vegetables to stove and thicken with butter-and-flour mixture, whisking while the broth simmers. Add pheasant meat back to broth. Add cooked rice and frozen corn, add salt and pepper to taste, and finish with heavy cream.

Serve hot with fresh bread.

Chef John Noel Gilbertson, CEC, Spring Lake Hunting Lodge and Resort, Oldham, South Dakota

Venison Loin with Vermouth and Dried Fruits

serves four to six

1 tablespoon (15 ml) vegetable oil

2 pounds (0.9 kg) fresh venison loin cutlets,
   cut 1-inch (2.5 cm) thick

Salt and pepper

1 cup (120 g) dried cranberries,
   blueberries, raisins, or cherries

1 cup (235 ml) red sweet vermouth

1 cup (235 ml) veal or beef broth

2 tablespoons (56 g) cold butter, cubed

Salt and coarse pepper

Heat oil in a large (12-inch/30 cm) frying pan over high heat until barely smoking.

Season cutlets with salt and pepper. Add seasoned cutlets to hot oil and sauté each side until browned. Transfer venison to a cutting board and cover loosely with foil to keep warm.

Add dried fruit, vermouth, and broth to pan and reduce by three-fourths. Vigorously whisk in cold butter, then add venison back into sauce and rewarm all ingredients. Adjust seasonings.

Serve immediately with a rice blend, potatoes au gratin, or other accompaniments.

Chef John Noel Gilbertson, CEC, Spring Lake Hunting Lodge and Resort, Oldham, South Dakota

Lucky Duck

serves four

3 tablespoons (42 g) butter

3 tablespoons (36 g) sugar

⅓ cup (78 ml) white wine

⅓ cup (78 ml) orange juice

2 tablespoons (30 ml) raspberry or
blackberry vinegar

1½ cups (227 g) frozen blackberries,
thawed

1¼ cups (294 ml) beef stock

½ cup (120 ml) chicken stock

2 tablespoons (30 ml) cognac (or brandy)

1 tablespoon (15 ml) maple syrup

1 tablespoon (8 g) cornstarch mixed with
1 tablespoon (15 ml) cold water

1½ to 2 pounds (675 to 900 g) duck
breasts, skin on

¼ cup (36 g) fresh blackberries, or frozen
whole blackberries, thawed

Melt butter in saucepan over medium-high heat. Add sugar and whisk until golden brown. Add white wine, orange juice, and vinegar and bring to boil. Add blackberries, beef stock, and chicken stock. Simmer until reduced by half. Strain through a wire mesh strainer, scraping and pushing berries into the strainer to extract juices and pulp. Pour into a clean saucepan and add cognac and maple syrup. Bring to a boil. Remove from heat, add cornstarch mixture, and whisk thoroughly. Return to heat and whisk while returning mixture to a boil. Cook for 1 minute, whisking constantly. Cover and keep warm until ready to serve.

Place the duck breasts skin-side down on a cutting board and trim all exposed excess fat so that only the fat directly below the breast meat remains. Using a very sharp knife, trim away any remaining tissue on the breast other than meat. Turn the duck breasts over and score the fat in a ¼-inch (6 mm) diamond pattern without slicing the meat. A very sharp knife is the key.

Preheat oven to 450°F (232°C). Heat a large (12-inch/ 30 cm) cast-iron frying pan over high heat. When pan is very hot, add duck, skin-side down. Reduce heat to medium-high. After 5 minutes, when most of the fat is rendered and the skin is nicely browned, flip the duck breasts over in the pan and continue cooking for 3 more minutes. Transfer the pan with the duck to oven for 3 minutes. Remove from oven and place duck breasts on cutting board. The duck breasts should be cooked to medium, with a pink center. Let stand 4 minutes.

To serve, spoon some warmed sauce onto individual dinner plates. Carve duck breasts on the bias into ¼-inch (6.4 mm) slices. Fan breast slices over sauce. Place a few fresh blackberries over duck slices. Drizzle a little more sauce over duck and blackberries and serve.

Tall Timber Lodge and Log Cabins, Pittsburg, New Hampshire

TALL TIMBER LODGE AND LOG CABINS, Pittsburg, New Hampshire

Bison Osso Buco

serves six

Salt and pepper
6 (12- to 16-ounce/340 to 454 g) bison
  shanks
Olive oil
2 large yellow onions, peeled and chopped
1 bunch celery, chopped
2 carrots, peeled and chopped
2 tablespoons (18 g) minced garlic
1 cup (235 ml) red wine
½ cup (120 ml) tomato paste
8 cups (2 liters) chicken or veal stock
Lemon zest for garnish
Chopped parsley for garnish

Preheat large roasting pan on stovetop burner. While pan is heating, generously rub salt and pepper on all sides of shanks. Add enough olive oil to bottom of roasting pan to coat it. Carefully place shanks in pan and sear on each side until brown. Remove shanks from pan and set aside.

Pour excess oil from pan and sauté onions, celery, carrots, and garlic until vegetables are tender. Add wine and use a wooden spoon to scrape up browned bits sticking to pan bottom. Add tomato paste and stock and mix well. Return shanks to pan. (There should be enough liquid in pan to go at least halfway up sides of shanks. If not, add some more stock.) Cover pan with foil and bake for at least 4 to 5 hours, turning shanks at least once.

After shanks are done cooking, remove from pan and set aside. Return roasting pan to stovetop and reduce liquid by at least half (the more you reduce it, the richer the sauce). Taste and adjust seasonings if necessary.

To serve, place bison shanks on plates and spoon sauce onto shanks. Garnish with lemon zest and chopped parsley. Creamy polenta and seasoned mashed potatoes make nice accompaniments.

Chef Curtis Falkenberg, Vermejo Park Ranch, Raton, New Mexico

VERMEJO PARK RANCH, Raton, New Mexico

Green Chili Stew

serves eight to ten

2 pounds (0.9 kg) green chilies (hot,
  medium, or mild), seeded and cored

1 tablespoon (15 ml) vegetable oil

6 cups (1.4 liters) chicken stock

1 pound (450 g) your choice of game meat
  (or chicken, pork, or beef), cubed, with
  fat trimmed away

1 medium yellow onion, diced

1 (8-ounce/227 g) can diced stewed
  tomatoes with juice

1 clove garlic, minced

1 teaspoon (1 g) dried oregano

2 russet potatoes, peeled and diced

Dash of liquid smoke

Preheat oven to 375°F (190°C). Toss chilies with oil to coat. Spread out on a baking sheet and roast chilies in oven for 25 to 30 minutes or until tender. Cool and chop roughly.

In large stockpot, bring chicken stock to simmer. Add chilies, meat, onion, tomatoes, garlic, and oregano. Simmer for 30 minutes. Add potatoes and liquid smoke and simmer for another 30 minutes or until meat is cooked and tender.

Chef Curtis Falkenberg, Vermejo Park Ranch, Raton, New Mexico

Bourbon Bread Pudding

serves serves ten to twelve

3 eggs

2 cups (400 g) plus 1 tablespoon (12 g)
    sugar, divided

1 cup (235 ml) plus ½ cup (120 ml)
    heavy cream, divided

1 tablespoon (15 ml) plus 1 teaspoon
    (5 ml) vanilla, divided

½ large (approximately 1 pound/450 g)
    Italian bread loaf, torn into 1-inch
    (2.5 cm) cubes

8 tablespoons (112 g) unsalted butter

¼ cup (60 ml) bourbon

Preheat oven to 350°F (180°C). In a mixing bowl, whisk eggs, add 1 cup (200 g) sugar, and continue whisking until mixed well. In a saucepan, combine 1 cup (235 ml) cream and 1 tablespoon (15 ml) vanilla and bring to a boil. Immediately remove pan from heat. Slowly pour the hot cream mixture into the egg mixture while whisking constantly.

Place bread cubes in a large bowl and pour cream mixture over cubes, allowing liquid to be absorbed. Transfer to 9 x 12-inch (23 x 30 cm) pan and bake for 45 to 60 minutes, or until the top is golden brown.

Meanwhile, in a separate saucepan, heat butter until melted. Whisk in 1 cup (200 g) sugar, then add bourbon. Simmer, but do not boil. Remove from heat and cool at room temperature until bread pudding is done. Remove bread pudding from oven, allow it to cool for about 10 minutes, then pour half the sauce over the pudding.

Whip remaining ½ cup heavy cream until frothy. Add 1 tablespoon (12 g) sugar and 1 teaspoon (5 ml) vanilla and continue whipping until soft peaks form.

To serve, scoop out generous portions of still-warm bread pudding onto dessert plates, ladle more warm sauce on top, and finish with a dollop of whipped cream.

Chef Tim Underwood, Wynfield Plantation, Albany, Georgia

WYNFIELD PLANTATION, Albany Georgia

Fried Quail with Honey-Tabasco Glaze

serves four to eight

Glaze

1 cup (235 ml) orange blossom (or other)
    honey
1 cup (235 ml) Tabasco or other hot red
    pepper sauce
2 tablespoons (12 g) Creole seasoning

Quail

Oil for frying
1 cup (235 ml) buttermilk
1 cup (235 ml) milk
½ cup (120 ml) Tabasco or other hot red
    pepper sauce
8 fresh quail
2 cups (250 g) flour
2 tablespoons (18 g) kosher salt
2 tablespoons (12 g) ground black pepper
2 tablespoons (70 g) granulated garlic

Combine all glaze ingredients.

In large, heavy-bottomed pot, pour oil 4 inches (10 cm) deep. Heat to 350°F (180°C), or until a piece of bread tossed into the oil begins frying in a second or two.

Meanwhile, preheat oven to 400°F (200°C).

In a large bowl, mix buttermilk, milk, and hot red pepper sauce, then add quail and toss to coat with mixture.

In another bowl, combine flour, salt, pepper, and garlic. Dredge quail, one at a time, in flour mixture, then dip again into buttermilk mixture, then into flour mixture again. Carefully lower 1 or 2 battered quail into hot oil and fry 4 to 5 minutes or until lightly golden brown. Remove from oil and drain on paper towels. Repeat with remaining quail.

Brush some of the glaze over the drained quail. Transfer to baking sheet and bake in oven for 10 minutes. Remove, glaze a second time, and serve immediately.

Best served with stone-ground grits and a vegetable.

Chef Tim Underwood, Wynfield Plantation, Albany, Georgia

Garlic-Butter Asparagus

serves four as a side dish

2 quarts (2 liters) water

2 tablespoons (18 g) salt for blanching water

1 pound (450 g) asparagus, washed and trimmed

4 tablespoons (56 g) butter, melted

1 clove garlic, minced

1 teaspoon (6 g) kosher salt

1 teaspoon (2 g) pepper

¼ cup (14 g) chopped fresh parsley

In a large pan, bring 2 quarts (2 liters) water to a rapid boil. Add 2 tablespoons (18 g) salt. Add asparagus and blanch for 2 to 3 minutes until tender, firm to the bite, and still green. Transfer to a large bowl of ice water to stop the cooking. Drain and dry asparagus. In a large (12-inch/30 cm) frying pan set on medium, melt butter and add garlic, salt, pepper, and parsley. Cook until aromatic. Add asparagus and warm through for 5 minutes. Serve with favorite game dish.

Chef Tim Underwood, Wynfield Plantation, Albany, Georgia

Ranch- and Farm-Raised Game Meats

- *If game is ranched, it is done so under free-range conditions. The animals roam over hundreds of acres and forage for their food. Because the animal is traveling for food, it is more exercised. This results in the animals having less body fat, giving the meat a more complex flavor.*
- *Farm-raised game are fed grains like wheat, alfalfa, or corn. Since these animals do not have to travel for food, and the food does not comprise a variety of wild vegetation, farmed game is milder in flavor and has more fat.*

Stone-Ground Cheddar Grits

serves four to six as a side dish

½ pound (224 g) butter

1 small onion, diced

2 tablespoons (36 g) salt

1 tablespoon (6 g) ground black pepper

1 tablespoon (35 g) granulated garlic

1 cup (235 ml) water

1 cup (235 ml) milk

1 cup (235 ml) heavy cream

1 cup (156 g) grits

1 cup (113 g) shredded cheddar cheese

In a 4- to 6-quart (3.8 to 5.7 liter) saucepan set on medium-high heat, add the butter, onion, salt, pepper, and granulated garlic. Cook until onion is translucent. Add water, milk, and heavy cream and bring to a simmer. Add grits and whisk for 20 minutes while simmering. Add shredded cheddar cheese and add more salt and pepper, if needed.

Chef Tim Underwood, Wynfield Plantation, Albany, Georgia

Hunting Lodges Directory

Amangani Resort, Jackson, Wyoming

Amangani Resort

Amangani, which means "peaceful home," enjoys a unique location with panoramic views of the Teton Peaks and Snake River Range and is within easy access to Yellowstone's two national parks. This luxury resort brings hunters a unique experience. The call of the bull elk is heard throughout the region during the September–October mating season. Amangani arranges private trips to Jenny Lake, a favored spot for mating elks. Hunting seasons for elk, deer, and waterfowl are generally open from September until December. Though strictly regulated, black bears, mountain lions, and other trophy species are also hunted.

1535 North East Butte Road
Jackson, Wyoming 83001
877.734.7333
www.amanresorts.com

BIG HOLE C4 LODGE, Twin Bridges, Montana

Big Hole C4 Lodge

The Big Hole C4 Lodge and its surrounding lands offer a remarkable adventure for hunters. All hunts are non guided to ensure guests' full independence. Hunt large game or wing shoot.

80 Ultley Lane
Twin Bridges, Montana 59754
877.684.5760
www.bigholec4lodge.com

The Lodge and Ranch at Chama Land and Cattle Company

Chama offers hunters a wide array of species, including mule deer, Merriam's turkey, American bison, and elk. Surrounded by 36,000 acres (14500 ha), the lodge offers world-class facilities and cuisine, making it one of the premier personal and corporate retreats in the world.

P.O. Box 127
Chama, New Mexico 87520
505.756.2133
www.lodgeatchama.com

Deer Creek Lodge

Offering over 14,000 acres (5600 ha) of pristine private property, Deer Creek has attained recognition as a worldwide hunting destination. Awarded the esteemed title of one of only twenty-four Orvis-endorsed wing-shooting lodges in the world, Deer Creek offers guests opportunities at upwards of 200 quail per day. Or opt to substitute a morning or afternoon of upland birds for a twenty-five-bird group limit of mallards. Unmatched pheasant, chukar, Hungarian partridge, wild turkey, dove, and trophy whitetail hunting. Sumptuous comfort is provided in a 10,000-square-foot (930 sq m) luxury lodge that opened in the fall of 2006.

8160 State Route 132 East
P.O. Box 39
Sebree, Kentucky 42455
888.875.3000
www.deercreekoutfitters.com

Dymond Lake Lodge, Thompson, Manitoba

Dymond Lake Lodge

This is Manitoba's most exclusive wing-shooting destination. Located just north of Churchill on the Hudson Bay Coast, Dymond Lake Lodge offers a unique waterfowling adventure and is situated among North America's main flyway and staging and feeding grounds. The hosts, having lived and operated in the area for the last thirty-five years, bring a wealth of experience that enables them to provide the ultimate wilderness adventure for their guests.

P.O. Box 425
Thompson, Manitoba
Canada, R8N 1N2
888.WEBBERS
www.webberslodges.com

Flowers River Lodge, Mt. Pearl, Newfoundland

Flowers River Lodge

Nestled between the majestic mountains of northern Labrador, 50 miles (80 km) inland from Flowers Bay, the Lodge is located in a stretch of wilderness that provides top-notch hunting. Labrador is home to the George River caribou herd, the largest in the world. In addition to fishing and hunting, the Flowers River area is a scenic haven for the eco-minded individual.

P.O. Box 92
Mt. Pearl, Newfoundland
Canada, A1N 2C1
877.SALMON4 (725.6664)
709.682.8663 (winter)
709.896.3901 (summer)
www.flowersriver.com

Flying B Ranch

This Orvis-endorsed wing-shooting lodge, located at the base of the Clearwater Mountain range, offers guests one of the largest land concessions in the state of Idaho for big game hunting of elk, whitetail and mule deer, black bear, cougar, bobcat, and moose. The Flying B Ranch holds exclusive outfitting rights to over 740,000 acres (300000 ha) of the Clearwater and Nez Perce National Forests under special use permit from the United States Forest Service.

2900 Lawyer Creek Road
Kamiah, Idaho 83536
800.472.1945
208.935.0755
www.flyingbranch.com

Golden Ranch Plantation

This 50,000-acre (20000 ha) plantation is located in the heart of Louisiana's Cajun country. The plantation house, built in the 1860s, serves as the main lodge for guests. Alligator hunting begins in September, followed by early quail season. November through January provides top-notch deer and duck action. The cool, yet pleasant, weather in February and March provides a great finish for the quail season. Continental pheasant shoots, available throughout the season, provide challenging wing shooting.

146 Coteau Ducypre
Gheens, Louisiana 70355
985.532.5221
www.goldenranch.com

GROSSE SAVANNE WATERFOWL AND WILDLIFE LODGE, Lake Charles, Louisiana

Grosse Savanne Waterfowl & Wildlife Lodge

Located in the southwest corner of Louisiana, Grosse Savanne is a luxury resort nestled in the heart of Cameron Parish County, easily accessible to Gulf of Mexico beaches, abundant wildlife and fisheries, and fresh- and saltwater marshes. This Orvis-endorsed wing-shooting lodge encompasses more than 50,000 acres (20000 ha) and hosts most species, including mallards, pintails, woods, gadwalls, and teals, as well as snows, blues, and speckle-belly. In addition, Grosse Savanne offers the thrill of an alligator hunt.

1730 Big Pasture Road
Lake Charles, Louisiana 70607
337.598.2357
www.grossesavanne.com

HEARTLAND WILDLIFE RANCHES Ethel, Missouri

Heartland Wildlife Ranches

Called one of North America's premier hunting destinations, Heartland Wildlife Ranches sportsmen will find whitetail, elk, red stag, turkey, and red sheep on 7,200 acres (3000 ha). With a 20,000-square-foot (1900 sq m) luxury lodge, hunters can unwind after a day of adventure.

Heartland Wildlife Ranch
18503 State Highway, VV
Ethel, Missouri 63539
888.590.HUNT
660.486.3215
www.heartland-wildlife.com

JOSHUA CREEK RANCH, *Boerne Texas*

Joshua Creek Ranch

Hunters can choose from quail, pheasant, chukar, and Hungarian partridge in a season that runs from October 1 through March 31. There are whitetail deer and the big rack axis, as well as Rio Grande turkey. In addition to a variety of game, there is an expansive array of bird hunts: traditional walk-up shooting with experienced bird dogs, European-style driven pheasant shooting, and continental pheasant shoot, where hunters and their dogs rotate through ten challenging stations with a variety of different terrain retrieves. Experienced guides know the land, the wildlife, and the essentials of hunting. They are at your side to instruct, if needed; to assist; or simply to find the birds and handle the dogs. A variety of wing-shooting packages and deer and turkey-hunting options are available, or a custom package can be developed.

P.O. Box 1946
132 Cravey Road
Boerne, Texas 830.537.5090
830.230.5190 San Antonio Metro
www.joshuacreek.com

KEYAH GRANDE, *Pagosa Springs, Colorado*

Keyah Grande

Husband-and-wife team Barbara and Alan Sackman own this 4,000-acre (1600 ha) luxury retreat where eight individual suites are each designed with a different country or region's theme, from Santa Fe to China. Keyah Grande caters to nature lovers on every level, as well as sportsmen who enjoy skeet and trap shooting, and a sporting clay range. For hunters, there are trophy elk on the property. At the end of the day's adventures, the dining room offers an array of gourmet cuisine with fresh ingredients that are provided by artisan producers and small farmers.

13211 Highway 160 West
Pagosa Springs, Colorado 81147
970.731.1160
www.keyahgrande.com

Lajitas, the Ultimate Hideout
Lajitas, Texas

Lajitas, the Ultimate Hideout

Tucked away in west Texas between Big Bend National Park and Big Bend State Park lies this 25,000-acre (10000 ha) private estate where a cast of infamous characters made history and the Old West inspires the rugged luxury of Texas's first destination resort. Row after row of milo, millet, and sunflower stalks attract an abundance of white-wing dove to the 650-acre (265 ha) Lajitas Hunt Club, with luxury bunkhouse accommodations. Half-day hunts and full-day hunts are available. Attendants carry the ammunition, pick up shell casings, clean the game, and are always available. White-wing dove hunts are available from September 1 through October 30 and December 26 through January 4. Blue quail hunting in the Big Bend with the finest guided hunts is available November through February. Practice your aim at Five Stand (skeet shooting) or Cowboy Action Shooting Range. Five Stand is a shotgun shooting game using sporting clays; the game allows shooters of all abilities some of the most exciting target combinations available in the world today. The course utilizes eight automatic traps to simulate game birds such as dove, quail, and pheasant and even a rabbit bolting across the ground. One round consists of twenty-five shots with groups of shots being taken from each shooting stand.

HC 70, Box 400
Lajitas, Texas 79852
432.424.5000
www.lajitas.com

Libby Camps, Sporting Lodges
and Outfitter, Ashland, Maine

Libby Camps Sporting Lodges and Outfitter

An Orvis-endorsed wing-shooting lodge, Libby Camps has been owned and operated by the same family for five generations. Today, owners Matt and Ellen Libby provide a unique hunting experience. Bear, moose, deer, grouse, and woodcock are all part of the Libby adventure. Eight simple cabins, handcrafted from peeled spruce and fir logs, lit by kerosene lamps and heated by woodstoves, are situated just back from the water. We offer exceptional Maine guides and home-cooked family-style meals. Lodge seaplanes access ten outpost camps, and there are eighty canoes and boats on over thirty different waters within a 20-mile (32 km) radius of camp. The camps are 45 miles (72 km) from the nearest town by private gravel road.

P.O. Box 810
Ashland, Maine 04732
207.435.8274
www.libbycamps.com

Lily Pond Creek Hunting Lodge
Jackson, North Carolina

Lily Pond Creek Hunting Lodge

In the Dock family for more than 100 years, Lily Pond is located in Northampton County, one of the top counties in the state for whitetail. It usually tops the charts on deer and bucks per square mile. The county is famous for growing peanuts, and the deer love them. Many hunters say the meat here tastes much better than any deer meat they have ever had, and Lily Pond owners credit the peanuts. Lily Pond enjoys the most liberal bag limit on deer and a long season. Bear and wild turkey are also hunted here.

P.O. Box 535
Jackson, North Carolina 27845
252.534.7381
www.lilypondcreek.com

The Resort at Paws Up,
Greenough, Montana

The Resort at Paws Up

Paws Up is a 37,000-acre (15000 ha) ranch nestled in the foothills of the Garnet Mountains in the heart of the Blackfoot Valley in Montana and offers an extraordinary upland bird-hunting experience. Guests work closely with their expert guide and pointer to locate and jump birds. At the conclusion of hunts, birds are processed and prepared to guest specifications. The nearby Blackfoot River is known worldwide due to its prominence in the best-selling novel *A River Runs Through It* by Norman Maclean, and the successful movie directed by Robert Redford and starring Brad Pitt.

40060 Paws Up Road
Greenough, Montana 59823
406.244.5200
866.894.7969
www.pawsup.com

Rio Piedra Plantation,
Camilla, Georgia

Rio Piedra Plantation

Orvis-endorsed, the Rio Piedra Plantation offers spectacular quail hunting. Guests explore classic South Georgia quail-hunting terrain for several miles along the majestic Flint River with knowledgeable guides and well-trained bird dogs. To assure a successful and traditional hunt, native quail are supplemented with superior-quality bobwhite quail, raised and early-released to covey like native birds. Packages range from half-day to three-day hunts. Individual packages arranged.

5749 Turkey Road
Camilla, Georgia 31730
800.538.8559
229.336.1677
www.riopiedraplantion.com

Rough Creek Lodge and Resort,
Glen Rose, Texas

Rough Creek Lodge & Resort

There's no roughing it at Rough Creek. It has been named Most Outstanding Lodge in America by Condé Nast Johansens and one of America's Top Restaurants for three years in a row by Zagat. This luxury resort is one of Dallas–Fort Worth's finest upland bird-hunting and Texas deer-hunting locations. Quail, chukar, and pheasant abound in the many hunting fields. Dove and turkey hunting are also offered during the Texas parks and wildlife seasons. Hundreds of additional acres of prime hunting land have been opened on the existing 11,000-acre (4500 ha) ranch to hunt feral hog and whitetail deer. Elk and exotics are available on neighboring ranches.

P.O. Box 2400
Glen Rose, Texas 76043
800.864.4705
www.roughcreek.com

Spring Lake Hunting Lodge
and Resort, Oldham, South Dakota

Spring Lake Hunting Lodge and Resort

Spring Lake Hunting Lodge offers some of the best wild pheasant, deer, and waterfowl hunting available. The emphasis is on fewer total hunters and superior shooting. Plenty of shooting and full limits are standard fare. Each hunt is customized according to the size and specific desires of the party.

44915 218th Street
Oldham, South Dakota 57051
605.482.9663
www.springlakehuntinglodgeandresort.com

Tall Timber Lodge and Log Cabins

Tall Timber Lodge has been Editor's Pick in *Yankee* magazine's Travel Guide to New England for four years in a row, and it has been chosen as one of four sporting lodges to visit in the United States by *Men's Journal* magazine. Built on the northern shore of Back Lake in 1946, it has become one of the most popular sporting lodges in all New England. Located in the heart of northern New Hampshire's unspoiled wilderness, Tall Timber is surrounded by the Connecticut Lakes, the headwaters of the Connecticut River, and many remote streams and ponds. Hunt here for ruffed grouse, woodcock, ring-necked pheasant, bear, and buck in 300 square miles (777 sq km) of forest.

609 Beach Road
Pittsburg, New Hampshire 03592
800.83.LODGE
www.talltimber.com

Vermejo Park Ranch

Whether you're trying to outwit the wary Merriam's gobbler, pursuing the fleet-footed pronghorn, searching for the elusive mule deer, or stalking the majestic bull elk, hunting at Vermejo Park Ranch is a memorable experience. It comprises 588,000 acres, (240000 ha) all owned and sustained by Ted Turner. While hunting and fishing are significant programs on the ranch, the main focus is the restoration and enhancement of the ranch's many diverse ecosystems.

P.O. Drawer E
Raton, New Mexico 87740
505.445.3097
www.vermejoparkranch.com

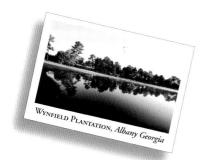

Wynfield Plantation

Wynfield Plantation, the Orvis 2004–2005 Wingshooting Lodge of the Year, is Georgia quail hunting at its best. Guests can hunt quail or enjoy bobwhite gunning. Hunt using your own dog or one of the highly trained bird dogs here. At Wynfield, guests have access to some of the finest shotguns and gun fitters and gunsmiths, ready to service the guns you may already own or to custom fit and build a shotgun specifically tailored for you. Wynfield offers traditional southern quail hunting in the sweet Georgia pines and scented sage grass.

Highway 62
PO Box 71686
Albany, Georgia 31708
229.889.0193
www.wynfieldplantation.com

Index

Photo Credits

Cover (center) Courtesy of The Resort at Paws Up

Page 13 Courtesy of Aman Resorts

Page 26 Courtesy of Big Hole C4 Lodge

Page 29 Courtesy of Lodge at Chama

Page 32 Tim Stull

Page 37 Courtesy of Dennis Fast

Page 40 Flowers River Lodge

Page 42 Courtesy of Flying B Ranch

Page 49 Golden Ranch Plantation

Page 50 Courtesy of Grosse Savanne Lodge

Page 55 Courtesy of Joshua Creek Ranch

Page 60 Courtesy of Lajitas, The Ultimate Hideout

Page 62 Courtesy of Libby's Sports Lodges

Page 66 Courtesy of Lily Pond Creek Hunting Lodge

Page 68 Courtesy of The Resort at Paws Up

Page 69 Courtesy of Rio Piedra Plantation

Page 73 Courtesy of Rough Creek Lodge & Resort

Page 96 Courtesy of Spring Lake Hunting Lodge

Page 106 Mickey Deneher

Page 107 Courtesy of Vermejo Park Ranch

Page 110 Courtesy of Wynfield Plantation

Creative Publishing international

is your complete source for fish and wild game cookbooks.